HOT BUTTONS
on
DISCIPLESHIP

HOT BUTTONS

on

DISCIPLESHIP

Going Deep, Growing Strong, and Standing Firm

by
Frank R. Shivers

LIGHTNING SOURCE
1246 Heil Quaker Blvd.
La Vergne, TN

Unless otherwise noted, Scripture quotations are from
The Holy Bible *King James Version*

Library of Congress Cataloging-in-Publication Data

Shivers, Frank R., 1949–
Hot Buttons on Discipleship / Frank Shivers
ISBN 978-1-878127-16-7

Library of Congress Control Number:
2012900130

Cover design by
Tim King of Click Graphics, Inc.

For Information:
Frank Shivers Evangelistic Association
P. O. Box 9991
Columbia, South Carolina 29290
www.frankshivers.com

To

Glen Hughes

A Faithful Friend

Content

Preface

There are three kinds of men (1 Corinthians 2:14–3:1). The **natural man** is he who is dead in trespasses and sin and blind to either the reality or need of Christ.

The **carnal man,** though saved, lives a life centered on the appetites of the flesh to the neglect of that which is spiritual. Disobedient, thus *dwarfed,* this believer fails to grow, mature, or develop spiritually.

He is a *defeated* Christian, not knowing the victory that walking under the control of the Holy Spirit enables, and is dependent upon another to do for him what he cannot or will not do spiritually—like a baby is dependent upon its parent.

Further, the carnal Christian is a *disappointing* Christian, failing to live up to God's design. Sadly, many students fit into this category.

The **spiritual man** is the believer who lives under the control and dominion of the Holy Spirit. This believer continuously crucifies the lusts of the flesh, the lust of the eyes, and the pride of life, denying self to the pleasure of the Lord.

Discipleship is following Christ and growing in His likeness, as one sees in the spiritual man. *Hot Buttons on Discipleship*, the third volume in the Hot Button series for students, is purposed to assist the believer in this quest.

To assure comprehension and application, each Hot Button is concluded with an Ask Yourself section for personal and group discussion.

The Christian life means living in the two halves of reality: the supernatural and the natural parts. I would suggest that it is perfectly possible for a Christian to be so infiltrated by twentieth-century [twenty-first century] thinking that he lives most of his life as though the supernatural were not there....Being a biblical Christian means living in the supernatural now.[1]—Francis Schaeffer

The yielding of our members as instruments (Romans 6:13) is abandoning all control over our service as to *place, time, or quality.* Its formula is "anything, anytime, anywhere." The point of emphasis is the *utterness* of the abandonment of our bodies to Him.[2]—C. I. Scofield

Do not wait until your experience has ripened into maturity before you attempt to serve God. Endeavour now to bring forth fruit.[3]—C. H. Spurgeon

The battle may take one minute or a year; that will depend on me, not on God. But it must be wrestled out alone before God, and I must resolutely go through the hell of a renunciation before Him. Nothing has any power over the man who has fought out the battle before God and won there.[4]—Oswald Chambers

1   Not for Sale

"For what is a man profited, if he shall gain the whole world, and lose his own soul? or what shall a man give in exchange for his soul?"—Matthew 16:26.

I would rather die for Christ than rule the whole earth. Leave me to the beasts that I may by them be a partaker of God.[5]—Ignatius (who was thrown to the beasts in the Coliseum in Rome)

> This heart belongs to Jesus; He saved my soul from Hell.
> This heart belongs to Jesus; oh, this heart is not for sale.
> Not for sale, not for sale, no way, no sir;
> Not for sale, I'm not for sale![6]—Michael Combs

You are either up for sale or not for sale. Some up-for-sale characters in Scripture include

- Eve, who sold a paradise home for a bite of fruit
- Esau, who sold his birthright for a bowl of beans
- King David, who sold his testimony and purity for an adulterous affair with Bathsheba
- King Saul, who sold his kingdom for some forbidden spoils of war
- Samson, who sold his spiritual power for a night with Delilah
- The "rich fool," who sold his soul for a new storage warehouse full of possessions he soon lost
- Judas, who sold Jesus out for thirty pieces of silver, the price of a slave

Each of these sold to the Devil and the world what never should have been up for sale to begin with.

What do you have in your life that is not for sale even to the highest bidder—things that are absolutely non-negotiable, not for sale at any price; things you will go to the wall for; things you will die for? I hope you will join me in saying, first of all, "MY FAITH IS NOT FOR SALE."

Polycarp refused to sell Jesus out. The proconsul asked him if he were Polycarp. When he assented, the former counseled him to deny Christ, saying, "Consider thyself, and have pity on thy own great age" and many other such-like speeches which they are wont to make. The proconsul then urged him, saying, "Swear, and I will release thee—reproach Christ."

Polycarp answered, "Eighty and six years have I served him, and He never once wronged me; how then shall I blaspheme my King, Who hath saved me?"

The proconsul again urged him, "Swear by the fortune of Caesar."

Polycarp replied, "Since you still vainly strive to make me swear by the fortune of Caesar, as you express it, affecting ignorance of my real character, hear me frankly declaring what I am. I am a Christian, and if you desire to learn the Christian doctrine, assign me a day, and you shall hear."

Hereupon the proconsul said, "I have wild beasts, and I will expose you to them, unless you repent."

"Call for them," replied Polycarp.

"I will tame thee with fire," said the proconsul, "since you despise the wild beasts, unless you repent."

Then said Polycarp, "You threaten me with fire which burns for an hour and is soon extinguished, but the fire of the future judgment and of eternal punishment reserved for the ungodly you are ignorant of. But why do you delay? Do whatever you please."

The proconsul sent the herald to proclaim thrice in the middle of the stadium, "Polycarp hath professed himself a Christian." The people gathered wood to burn him at the stake.

Polycarp's last words were: "O Father, I bless thee that thou hast counted me worthy to receive my portion among the martyrs."

Polycarp's love for Christ was not for sale even for the price of life itself. Resolve to be a Polycarp and go to the wall in defense of the faith in Jesus Christ.

Don't sell the Faith out to fly-by-night religions that spring up. You have the Truth. Stick with it regardless of cost or consequence. James Harper, a choir member of the Grand Junction High School, Grand Junction, Colorado, took an unpopular stand when he refused to sing a song of praise to Allah. Lyrics in the song included, "There is no truth like Allah," and "Allah is the only eternal and immortal." Harper said, "This is worshipping another god, and even worshipping another prophet—I think there would be a lot of outrage if we made a Muslim choir say Jesus Christ is the only truth."[7] Harper refused to cower down to peer pressure and utter words that denounced the very God he loved and served. He is an example of a Christian taking a stand, even when it meant standing alone.

Second, join me in saying loudly, "MY BIBLE IS NOT FOR SALE." Martin Luther told the Roman Catholic Church that the Bible was not for sale. Despite threats of punishment if he did not recant his belief, he said, "My conscience is the prisoner to the Word of God. I cannot and will not recant. Here I stand; I can do none other. God help me." This stand resulted in his excommunication by the pope and condemnation as an outlaw by the emperor.

Don't sell the Bible out for the heretical views of a professor, teacher, or friend. Dr. R. A. Torrey offers timely advice in stating, "The truly wise man is he who believes the Bible against the opinions of any man, whether scientist, philosopher, or theologian.

If the Bible says one thing and any man or body of men say another thing, the truly wise man will say, 'The Bible is the Word of Him who cannot lie.'"

To insure the Bible is never up for sale, engage in four things with it.

Possess it. That is, know it, not simply tote it. Master the Bible as a lawyer would master a law manual, or a doctor a medical book. C. H. Spurgeon testified, "Cut me anywhere, and I bleed Bible."

Prize it. Discover the awesome treasure you have in the Bible in order to join David in saying, "Thy word is very pure: therefore thy servant loveth it." "I love thy commandments above gold; yea, above fine gold." "The law of thy mouth is better unto me than thousands of gold and silver" (Psalm 119:140, 127, 72). Delight in the Word.

Protect it. Be ever ready to give a reason for the hope that you possess in Christ Jesus to all who ask or challenge. Jude exhorts us to "earnestly contend for the faith" (verse 3).

Proclaim it. Flesh the Word out into conduct and conversation. We become more surefooted in the Word, the more we declare it.

A preacher once came to a city to win its people to Christ. At first, the people listened to his sermons, but they gradually drifted away until there was not a single soul to hear the preacher when he spoke. One day a traveler said to him, "Why do you go on preaching?"

The preacher replied, "In the beginning, I hoped to change these people. If I still shout, it is only to prevent them from changing me." We have to keep "shouting" the Truth to keep the world from changing us!

Next, join me in saying loudly and unashamedly, "MY CHURCH ALLEGIANCE IS NOT FOR SALE." It appears that a gigantic tent sale is happening with regard to the New Testament Church. Seventy-four percent of protestant teens state that the church is not important with regard to living a committed life for Christ. The writer of Hebrews clearly expresses God's mind and heart about the church in declaring, "You should not stay away from the church meetings, as some are doing, but you should meet together and encourage each other. Do this even more as you see the day coming" (Hebrews 10:25, NCV). Jesus loved the church and gave Himself for it. How much then ought we to do the same!

Can you be a Christian without joining the church? Yes, it is possible. It is something like being

A student who will not go to school
A soldier who will not join an army
A citizen who does not pay taxes or vote
A salesman with no customers
An explorer with no base camp
A seaman on a ship without a crew
A businessman on a deserted island
An author without readers
A tuba player without an orchestra
A parent without a family
A football player without a team
A politician who is a hermit
A scientist who does not share his findings
A bee without a hive[8]

Don't swap the church for a newfangled thing that surfaces. It is one of the two divine institutions He promises to bless.

Then join me in declaring, "MY PERSONAL HOLINESS IS NOT FOR SALE." It was said by one person, "Everything I have is for sale, if the price is right." Will you sell out your purity, wholesomeness, and testimony, if the price is right (money, fame, promotion) or to date Mr. or Miss Popular on campus? Have you already? Joseph, in Scripture, was not for sale, though Mrs. Potiphar relentlessly made solicitations. He said to her advances, 'I cannot do this great wickedness, and sin against God?" (Genesis 39:9). Make personal holiness nonnegotiable in your life.

Further, join me in saying loudly, "MY CHRISTIAN SERVICE IS NOT FOR SALE." Billy Graham felt his call to evangelism was not for sale. Upon being offered a position in the Nixon White House, Graham immediately refused, saying, "You could not offer me a job as ambassador or a cabinet post that I would give a second thought to. When God called me to preach, it was for life." God's call upon your life is nonnegotiable and must not be renounced, regardless of cost or consequence. Is it that God has called you to be a missionary, pastor, evangelist, chaplain, student minister, or music minister? If so, you can do anything but turn back from the call!

Every month 1,600 ministers depart the ministry. Fifty percent of students in seminary today will be out of the ministry in five years. Far too many are selling out their call for worldly pleasure or possessions. Bill Borden's parents did not welcome the news that God had called him to missionary service and severed financial support. Disap-pointed in their response but not discouraged, he went to the mission field. Sadly, he was only on the mission field for a short time before contracting an illness that led to his death. Found in his room on the mission field was a note that stated, "No retreat. No regret." With Borden, firmly resolve not to retreat from God's call, regard-less of the price required.

Jesus said, "People will insult you and hurt you. They will lie and say all kinds of evil things about you because you follow me. But when they do, you will be blessed. Rejoice and be glad, because you have a great reward waiting for you in heaven. People did the same evil things to the prophets who lived before you" (Matthew 5:11–12 NCV). Billy Graham said, "Courage is contagious. When a brave man takes a stand, the spines of others are often stiffened.[9]

6

You shouldn't be surprised when you are mistreated or misunderstood for standing up for Christian values. Jesus was. In fact, Jesus emphatically states that persecution will come to His followers. "If the world hate you, ye know that it hated me before it hated you. If ye were of the world, the world would love his own: but because ye are not of the world, but I have chosen you out of the world, therefore the world hateth you" (John 15:18–19). Frankly, if the world (demonic world system) fails to present trouble, then most likely you're not standing as tall as you should for Christ.

As Hugh Latimer and Nicholas Ridley were both about to be burned as heretics for their teachings and beliefs outside Balliol College, Oxford (16 October 1555), Latimer exclaimed, "Be of good comfort, Master Ridley, and play the man! We shall this day light such a candle, by God's grace, in England, as I trust shall never be put out."[10] In facing persecution for mirroring Christian values and expressing the faith, "Play the man," lighting a fire on campus, athletic field, and job for Christ that no man can extinguish. Don't cower down. Never be ashamed of Christ. Take the ribbing and rejection. Never recant your beliefs. (Romans 1:16)

Also, join me in saying, "MY DEVOTIONAL TIME IS NOT FOR SALE." King Darius decreed that no man in his kingdom could pray to any god for thirty days upon penalty of death. Daniel hung out his "NOT FOR SALE" sign on his bedroom door and prayed as usual. Are you selling out devotional time with the Lord for television, recreation, sleep, or the computer?

Last, join me in saying, "MY WITNESSING IS NOT FOR SALE." It is said that when General William Booth lay dying, he was asked for a message to send around the world. With his dying breath, he uttered that the message should be—others. This one-word message summed up the life and ministry of this great soul winner. Others need our witness. Others need to be reached for Christ. Others need to hear the Gospel of the Lord Jesus Christ. Others need cleansing of sin. Others need peace with God. Others need meaning and fulfillment in life. Others must be warned about the reality of Hell. Others must be told of the hope of Heaven. It is when we shift our eyes from self to others that God can use us to win souls.

"But Peter and John replied, 'Do you think God wants us to obey you rather than him? We cannot stop telling about everything we have seen and heard.'" (Acts 4:19 NLT). With Peter and John, say the same to all who would have you be quiet about Christ. Declare "My lips are not up for sale. They will never cease telling of Jesus' love for the world."

At the beginning of the twentieth century, Christians taking the Gospel to China met violent resistance from Chinese rebels (Boxer Rebellion). A mission school housing students studying for the ministry was attacked. The rebels offered freedom to every student who would trample over a cross laid at the school's only unblocked exit; the others would be shot. The first six students who walked out trampled over the cross to their freedom. The seventh student, a teenage girl, walked up to the cross and knelt down by it as to pray for added strength, and then walked around it, only to meet her death in refusal to sell out. The remaining ninety-two students, infused by her faith and courage, did the same. Oh, the power of a righteous and courageous life to incite others to stand their ground for Christ regardless of cost or consequence!

Found among the papers of a young African pastor in Zimbabwe after he was martyred was discovered this brazen statement.

"I'm a part of the fellowship of the unashamed. The die has been cast. I have stepped over the line. The decision has been made. I'm a disciple of His, and I won't look back, let up, slow down, back away, or be still.

"My past is redeemed. My present makes sense. My future is secure. I'm finished with low living, sight walking, small planning, smooth knees, colorless dreams, tamed visions, mundane talking, cheap living, and dwarfed goals.

"I no longer need preeminence, prosperity, position, promotions, plaudits, or popularity. I don't have to be right or first or tops or recognized or praised or rewarded. I live by faith, lean on His presence, walk by patience, lift by prayer, and labor by the Holy Spirit's power.

"My face is set. My gait is fast. My goal is Heaven. My road may be narrow, my way rough, my companions few; but my guide is reliable, and my mission is clear.

"I will not be bought, compromised, detoured, lured away, turned back, deluded, or delayed.

"I will not flinch in the face of sacrifice or hesitate in the presence of the adversary. I will not negotiate at the table of the enemy, ponder at the pool of popularity, or meander in the maze of mediocrity.

"I won't give up, shut up, or let up, until I have stayed up, stored up, prayed up, paid up, and preached up for the cause of Christ.

"I am a disciple of Jesus. I must give until I drop, preach until all know, and work until He comes. And when He does come for His own, He'll have no problems recognizing me. My colors will be clear!"[11]

Will you join the young African pastor and me in saying to the Devil and the world, "I will NOT sell out" regardless of cost or consequence?

ASK YOURSELF

What biblical characters undoubtedly were up for sale due to their eventual fall?

What are the six areas that define the Christian and should not be up for sale at any price?

What price did Polycarp pay for refusing to sell out Jesus?

Do you know a Christian who sold out Jesus? In what way(s)?

Imagine you were one of the 100 Christian students entrapped in the mission school and challenged to trample over the cross. What would have you done?

Have you sold Jesus out for pleasure, popularity or possessions?

Using the Internet, Google Michael Combs' song *Not for Sale* on youtube.com and meditate over the lyrics as it is sung.

2   The Neglected Vineyard

"They made me the keeper of the vineyards; but mine own vineyard have I not kept."—Song of Solomon 1:6.

No spiritual discipline is more important than the intake of God's Word. Nothing can substitute for it. There simply is no healthy Christian life apart from a diet of the milk and meat of Scripture.[12]—Donald S. Whitney

The person speaking in this text had the responsibility for the upkeep (the pruning, plowing, planting) of vineyards that belonged unto others. It is clear from the text that she was not negligent in this assignment but diligent and determined to keep them so that each would fulfill its purpose to the owner's pleasure. Such faithfulness to her lord (the owner) and sacrificial work is commendable!

However, the passion that led her to serve so zealously in the vineyards of others caused her to neglect her own vineyard, and for that she should be reprimanded. This servant testifies, "They made me the keeper of the vineyards; but mine own vineyard have I not kept." She enabled the vineyards of others to stay pruned and thus bear much fruit, while her own was overtaken with weeds and thorns yielding little or no fruit.

Spiritually, this is true for many students. While they may be good at doing their God-given assignments in discipling another, teaching, singing, playing in a Christian band, starting a Bible club on campus, witnessing, or helping someone who is hurting that they are negligent of the work in the vineyard of their own heart! They "shine" outwardly but not inwardly. They promote the growth of others spiritually, while they remain stunted. The sorrowful words of the lady of our text is true for them. God "made me the keeper of the vineyards; but mine own vineyard have I not kept."

J. I. Packer states, "We have been brought to the point where we both can and must get our life's priorities straight. From current Christian publications, you might think that the most vital issue for any real or would-be Christian in the world today is church union or social witness or dialogue with other Christians and other faiths or refuting this or that ism or developing a Christian philosophy and culture or what have you. But our line of study makes the present-day concentration on these things look like a gigantic conspiracy of misdirection. Of course, it is not that; the issues themselves are real and must be dealt with in their place. But it is tragic that, in paying attention to them, so many in our day seem to have been distracted from what was and is and always will be the true priority for every human being—that is, learning to know God in Christ."[13]

S. D. Gordon stated, "A life of victory and power hinges upon three things: one, an act; two, a purpose; three, a habit—an initial act, a fixed purpose, a daily habit."[14] In sequence as stated, Gordon was referencing surrender, obedience, and quiet time. Gordon, in emphasizing the daily habit of quiet time, said, "After the initial act of surrender, the secret of a strong winsome Christian life is in spending time daily alone with God over His Word."

Start today the great work of pruning, plowing, and planting in the vineyard of *your* heart through disciplined resolve to daily study God's Word and pray, regularly prune the weeds of sin from your heart, and habitually attend church to receive biblical instruction and to be spurred forward by the saints in godliness. Top priority in your spiritual walk is to know God intimately through His Son, the Lord Jesus Christ.

ASK YOURSELF

What was the great mistake of the woman in this lesson? Why?

Do you think it is easy for a believer to become so occupied with duty that he neglects devotion?

Has this ever happened to you?

What safeguards are there to insure such neglect never happens?

On the other side of the issue, is it equally a danger that some will tend their own vineyard to the neglect of others? Explain.

Do you agree with J. I. Packer's assessment of the top priority of the Christian life? Why or why not?

3   Essentials to Effective Quiet Times

"My voice shalt thou hear in the morning, O LORD; in the morning will I direct my prayer unto thee, and will look up."—Psalm 5:3.

He who fritters away the early morning, its opportunity and freshness, in other pursuits than seeking God will make poor headway seeking Him the rest of the day. If God is not first in our thoughts and efforts in the morning, He will be in the last place the remainder of the day. Behind this early rising and early praying is the ardent desire which presses us into this pursuit after God. Morning listlessness is the index to a listless heart. The heart which is behind in seeking God in the morning has lost its relish for God.[15]—E. M. Bounds

To be a developed (mature), not distorted (malformed), believer requires time spent regularly in the presence of God. Obviously a daily quiet time is not to be approached out of a legalistic spirit so as to escape guilt, but with a loving heart longing to "know him, and the power of his resurrection, and the fellowship of his sufferings, being made conformable unto his death" (Philippians 3:10). Practice a quiet time not *in order* to have a relationship with God, but because you *have* a relationship with God; not out of "have to," but out of "want to." Five essential things need be observed to have a meaningful, beneficial quiet time.

The Right Spot

Select a place free from interruption where heart focus can be upon Holy God. Distraction is fatal. My favorite sacred spot is in my car at the park early in the morning; yours may be a nook in the library or the garage or the basement.

The Ready Soul

Exercise discipline to enter this time alertly, not when you are tired or fatigued. Enter it rightly, with sin confessed and heart clean. Enter it receptively, with mind open to hear and receive from the Lord.

The Regular Span

How much time ought you to spend in the quiet time on a regular basis? It should be time enough to include adoration and exaltation of God, mediation upon and digestion of Scripture, and supplication and intercession at God's throne in a beneficial manner. The secret to an effective devotional time is not the quantity of time but the quality of time.

The Required Stuff

In addition to a study Bible (Ryrie, The Open Bible, Scofield), a journal and a pen are needed to record truths learned, directives issued, and impressions gained. The palest ink is better than the most retentive memory, so write these things down.

The Routine Sequence

Start the quiet time with a brief prayer of praise and petition for illumination of His Word. Next, having predetermined the targeted Bible passage and with journal and pen in hand, initiate the study. In mediating upon the passage, search out six *Ps*: **place** where written, **person** by whom written, **people** to whom written, **purpose** for which written, **period** at which written, and then **personal** application for the truth taught.[16] George Mueller, the great London pastor, always gave precedence to the reading of the Word above time spent in prayer in his morning watches, and for good reason. Adrian Rogers stated, "It is more important for you to hear from God, than even for God to hear from you."[17] Read a Scripture passage repeatedly until its meaning and application are fully understood.

16

Internalize the truth learned through mediation. "Our souls," states C. H. Spurgeon, "are not nourished merely by listening awhile to this and then to that and then to the other part of divine truth. Hearing, reading, marking, and learning all require inwardly digesting to complete their usefulness, and the inward digesting of the truth lies for the most part in meditating upon it. Why is it that some Christians, although they hear many sermons, make but slow advances in the divine life? Because they neglect their closets and do not thoughtfully meditate on God's Word. They love the wheat, but they do not grind it; they would have the corn, but they will not go forth into the fields to gather it; the fruit hangs upon the tree, but they will not pluck it; the water flows at their feet, but they will not stoop to drink it. From such folly deliver us, O Lord."[18]

Engage in a time of supplication and intercession; then depart with readiness to obey what was received from the Lord. Share with a friend or family member what is internalized in the quiet time. Knowing others expect a report is an added motivation in its practice.

Spiritual growth hinges on daily communion with God—worship, intake of the Word, and prayer. And this takes discipline until it becomes a delight. In engaging the presence of God privately, soon you will say with David, "In thy presence is fulness of joy; at thy right hand there are pleasures for evermore" (Psalm 16:11).

In *Growing in Knowledge, Living by Faith,* I share numerous approaches to Bible study (theme, parable, miracle, book, etc.) that will prove valuable in charting a direction for a daily quiet time.

ASK YOURSELF

How important is it for the believer to practice a daily quiet time on a regular basis?

Explain the statement, "A believer engages in a quiet time not *in order* to have a relationship with God, but because he *has* a relationship."

Without looking back, what are the five essentials to an effective quiet time?

What ought to be given priority in the quiet time and why?

Six *P*s are listed for Bible study, the sixth of which is imperative. What is it?

How can you make the quiet time experience more effective?

Right now schedule a quiet time with the Lord for tomorrow and each day forward.

4   "Always to Pray, and Not to Faint"

"Men ought always to pray, and not to faint."—Luke 18:1.

The one concern of the Devil is to keep Christians from praying. He fears nothing from prayerless studies, prayerless work, and prayerless religion. He laughs at our toil, mocks at our wisdom, but he trembles when we pray.[19]—Samuel Chadwick

Four things let us ever keep in mind. God hears prayer, God heeds prayer, God answers prayer, and God delivers by prayer.[20]—E. M. Bounds

When prayer has become secondary, or incidental, it has lost its power. Those who are conspicuously men of prayer are those who use prayer as they use food or air or light or money.[21]—M. E. Andross

Prayer is conversation with God.

Jesus forthrightly issues the must of prayer in saying, "Men ought always to pray, and not to faint" (Luke 18:1). Believers live in an evil, polluted society. The only escape from its toxic fumes which promote spiritual fainting (drifting, backsliding, worldliness) is the intake of "pure air" from the atmosphere of Heaven which occurs in prayer. Prayer is to the believer what an oxygen mask is to those who work in hazardous waste facilities, an absolutely essential to survival. Obviously, then, this oxygen mask for believers ought to be worn continuously ("always to pray"). The apostle Paul similarly states, "Pray without ceasing" (1 Thessalonians 5:17).

Don't misunderstand what either Jesus or Paul is teaching. You are not being commanded to retire to a monastery and spend every waking hour in prayer on your knees. "Rather, it means," states Warren Wiersbe, "to make prayer as natural to us as our regular breathing. Unless we are sick or smothering, we rarely think about our breathing; we just do it. Likewise with prayer—it should be the natural habit of our lives, the 'atmosphere' in which we constantly live. Prayer is much more than the words of our lips; it is the desires of our hearts, and our hearts are constantly 'desiring' before Him, even if we never speak a word. So, to 'pray without ceasing' means to have such holy desires in our hearts, in the will of God, that we are constantly in loving communion with the Father, petitioning Him for His blessing."[22]

There are numerous times throughout the day when we should expressly pray, as cares, needs, and battles arise personally and with regard to others. All believers have experienced the prompting of the Holy Spirit to immediately stop their work or play to pray specifically for a friend, minister, or ministry. It's awesome to be so in tune with the Holy Spirit to hear His prompting to pray for someone, only later to learn that it was the channel through which God met a pressing need. Never delay praying for people when they are pressed to your heart by the Holy Spirit!

Christians should pray scripturally (in accordance with God's Word and will), passionately (earnestly, fervently), specifically (without vagueness), and confidently (not doubting, but fully trusting God to answer). Scripture indicates various postures of prayer: kneeling in prayer (1 Kings 8:54; 2 Chronicles 6:13; Psalm 95:6; Ephesians 3:14.); bowing and falling prostrate (Genesis 24:26, Matthew 26:39; Mark 14:35); spreading out the hands (1 Kings 8:22, Psalm 28:2; 1 Timothy 2:8); and standing (1 Samuel 1:26; Mark 11:25; Luke 18:11). No rule is specified with regard to the posture of the body in prayer. The only posture imperative in prayer is that of the heart. It must ever be kneeling in humility and submission in its approach to the throne room of a thrice holy God.

The Bible instructs us to pray in Jesus' name. The invoking of Jesus' name is not a magical formula. "Praying in Jesus' name," declares John MacArthur, "is not simply tacking a phrase onto the end of prayers. To pray in Jesus' name is to seek what He seeks, to promote what He desires, to give Him glory. We can only rightly ask God for that which will glorify the Son."[23]

Adrian Rogers comments, "When asking in Jesus' name, first consider: His Approval—Does Jesus approve this thing? His Authorization—Is it something He has authorized? His Acclaim—Is it for His glory?"[24]

Does prayer work? James states, "The earnest prayer of a righteous person has great power and produces wonderful results" (James 5:16 NLT). Sometimes prayer results are seen instantly, while at other times they are delayed. Sometimes we receive exactly that for which we pray, while at other times God provides something far better (though we may not think so at the time). Henry Drummond tells of a little girl aboard a ship en route across the ocean that dropped her doll overboard. She ran to the captain asking if he might stop the ship to rescue her doll. His refusal led her to count him insensitive and cruel. Upon reaching port, the captain purchased the finest doll available and gave it to the girl. He had refused her request but gave her something far better.[25] God always can be trusted "to do exceeding abundantly above all that we ask or think" (Ephesians 3:20).

The Prayer of Jabez

"And Jabez called on the God of Israel, saying, Oh that thou wouldest bless me indeed, and enlarge my coast, and that thine hand might be with me, and that thou wouldest keep me from evil, that it may not grieve me! And God granted him that which he requested."—1 Chronicles 4:10.

The prayer of Jabez reveals four specific things for which to pray. We should pray for **GRACE.** "Oh that thou wouldest bless me." Jabez prayed for divine enabling. The apostle Paul said, "But by the grace of God I am what I am: and his grace which was bestowed upon me was not in vain; but I laboured more abundantly than they all: yet not I, but the grace of God which was with me" (1 Corinthians 15:10). It is God's grace that enables us and equips us for effective service, not education, abilities, or charisma.

We should pray for **GROWTH.** Jabez prays, "Enlarge my coast," or my border, my territory of influence and service. Pray for God to enlarge, expand the coast of your influence and ministry opportunity. Pray for growth spiritually. Additionally pray that the ministry of the church and its pastoral staff, missionaries and evangelists will be enlarged.

We should pray for **GUIDANCE.** Jabez prayed, "That thine hand might be with me." The 'hand of God' is an expression that denotes the power of God in action. Pray for God's constant guidance regarding decisions to be made and directions to go (Psalm 139:5).

We should pray for **GODLINESS.** Jabez prayed, "That thou wouldest keep me from evil," that it may not pain me or that it might not spoil my life. Pray that God would keep you from sin and its painful consequences (Matthew 6:13). Pray to be holy and wholesome, free from the stain or stench of sin. Make your prayer that of Robert Murray McCheyne: "O God, make me as holy as a pardoned sinner can be."

The kind of praying that Jabez exhibited so impacted his life that he was called an honorable man by God (1 Chronicles 4:9).

Pray for all people. "I urge you, first of all, to pray for all people. Ask God to help them; intercede on their behalf, and give thanks for them" (1 Timothy 2:1 NLT). A daily prayer guide will help in fulfilling this obligation.

Monday—"M" pray for Ministers and Missionaries;

Tuesday—"T" pray for Troubled people who are experiencing trials and tribulation;

Wednesday—"W" pray for Workers with governing authority in the political arena;

Thursday—"T" pray for personal Tasks God has assigned you;

Friday—"F" pray for Friends and Foes;

Saturday—"S" pray for Sinners who need salvation and Saints who need revival;

Sunday—"S" pray for the Service of the church and those who preach, sing, and teach.

The prophet Daniel prayed regularly at set times and in a set place (Daniel 6:10). Make an appointment to meet God in prayer, scheduling the time and place each day. This is your "closet" prayer time. Plan the day around prayer, not prayer around the day. Prayer is to the believer's victory over sin and fellowship with God what oxygen is to our lungs. It is absolutely vital.

There is no such thing as unanswered prayer, just delayed answers to prayer.

ASK YOURSELF

Define prayer.

What is it to "pray without ceasing"?

What does it mean to "pray in Jesus name"?

In addition to praying scripturally, how else ought one to pray?

In what ways is the prayer of Jabez a prayer model?

Describe a time when the Holy Spirit prompted you to pray for someone, only afterward to learn that at the precise moment of your prayer, they were facing a crisis or great need.

For whom are you to pray?

How do you know that prayer really works (relate a personal experience and/or an experience of others).

5   The Abiding Life

"Abide in me, and I in you. As the branch cannot bear fruit of itself, except it abide in the vine; no more can ye, except ye abide in me." —John 15:4.

New Testament surrender is not a day, a week, a month, or a year. It is a contract for life. If you say you have surrendered your life to God, what are you doing off the altar?[26]—Stephen Olford

To live a victorious Christian life, the believer must constantly abide in Christ (John 15:5). To abide in Christ means to keep Him at the center of life, to obey Him without vacillating, to take cues from Him regarding decisions and conduct, and to steadfastly walk in intimacy with Him. Abiding in Christ requires serious diligence in the spiritual disciplines.

The two ways in which one can make tea illustrate the two methods of spiritual growth. The first is to boil water and dip the tea bag in and out of the water until it's ready. The second is to boil water and simply place the tea bag in the water until it is done. You don't want to be the type of believer who dips in and out of the church, Bible study, prayer, godliness, and fellowship with Christ. Your best growth will occur only when you abide (stay put) in the disciplines without wavering (John 15:4–7).

Envision a baseball glove on the ground. If a fly ball or grounder is hit right to the glove, could it make the catch? Obviously not. The glove cannot fulfill its purpose unless a baseball player's hand is in the glove. Properly fitted on a hand—abiding in it—that glove immediately becomes capable of anything the ballplayer can do. Your life is like the glove. Apart from the hand of God inserted in your life, it accomplishes nothing. However, with

God's hand abiding in the glove of your life, you can do anything God designs.

And just as dirt in a finger of the glove prevents the ball player from having full control in its use, dirt in the believer's life hinders God's use of his life. Keep the glove clean and well oiled for His use—24/7. You must "stay put" in Jesus to experience the victorious Christian life and the great and mighty things He will do through you.

ASK YOURSELF

What does it mean to abide in Christ?

Relate the illustration regarding the making of tea to the abiding life.

Relate the illustration cited about the baseball and glove to the abiding life.

What is promised to the believer who abides in Christ?

What is promised to the believer who does not?

Are you abiding in Christ?

6   The Why of the Church

"I was glad when they said unto me, Let us go into the house of the LORD."—Psalm 122:1.

Church attendance is as vital to a disciple as a transfusion of rich, healthy blood to a sick man.[27]—Dwight L. Moody

The church is the local assembly of baptized believers in Jesus Christ that has been divinely instituted for the advancement of the Gospel, edification of the saint, evangelization of the lost, exaltation of God, and implementation of God's teachings to the world. No campus ministry, Bible club, television evangelist, or Sunday iPod broadcast can substitute for the Christian's involvement in the local church. It was for the church that Jesus died.

Fifty-nine percent of students who profess to be Christians leave church life either permanently or for an extended period of time after age fifteen. Among reasons stated by teens for this departure is that the church is too judgmental, overprotective, exclusive, unfriendly toward doubters, and boring.[28] It is noteworthy that the same students state they had a very shallow Christian experience in church, which I believe identifies the root reason for their dropping out. Sadly, churches (not all) have disappointed students; but even in that, students yet ought to remain faithful to the church, due to the overarching fact of their love and devotion to Christ.

There are at least eight good reasons as to why students need to be faithfully involved in the ministry of a local New Testament church.

Go to Grow

Believers attend the Sunday school and worship services of the church in order to grow and abound in the things of God (Hebrews 10:25). Fresh servings of spiritual nutritional meat and potatoes are served regularly at the table of the local New Testament church to edify the believer and enhance growth in godliness and the will of God. Growth will be distorted if the believer fails to show up and eat up. The preaching and teaching of the Word received at church strengthens faith and walk aiding the spiritual maturing of the believer.

Go to Show

Dedication to a local church is a witness to the world of a believer's allegiance to Jesus Christ (Matthew 16:18). For one to speak of loving God and yet fail to obey Him in attendance at His house on the Lord's Day casts doubt upon their relationship to Him.

Go to Know

In the church, believers are aligned with people who love Jesus and spur each other onward in the Christian journey both in word and example (Acts 2:42). The giant redwoods, which have shallow root systems, withstand the force of mighty storms by intertwining their roots with those of other trees. Young believers in particular have shallow spiritual roots and will surely falter under Satanic assault, unless their roots are intertwined with those of mature believers in the church. Christian businessman Rich DeVos offers an imaginative picture of the fallacy of not fellowshipping with other believers. "Some people think of their spiritual life as if they were one person in a telephone booth talking to God on a private line. They don't want to be bothered by the demands of 'organized religion' and don't think they need anyone else. 'Oh, yeah, I'm spiritual,' they say; 'I just don't like church.' To those folks I say, 'You cannot grow spiritually in isolation.'"[29]

30

Go to Bestow

Scripture emphasizes the believer's need to join the Body of Christ in worship. David declares in Psalm 5:7, "But as for me, I will come into thy house in the multitude of thy mercy: and in thy fear will I worship toward thy holy temple." Psalm 149:1 exhorts, "Praise ye the LORD. Sing unto the LORD a new song, and his praise in the congregation of saints." A primary purpose in attending church is to engage in the corporate worship of God, bestowing on Him the sacrifice of praise and thanksgiving with lips of adoration. Worship is responding to God's graciousness, goodness, and being. Believers are to worship God with lip and life (externally and internally).

Go to Sow

The church is a place of service (Ephesians 2:10; Matthew 28:18–20). A person is not saved to laze around, but to get up and get going for God! In and through the varied evangelistic and missionary ministries of the church, believers can make a difference for eternity in the lives of others—locally, and even globally—by giving financially, witnessing, praying, and serving in various capacities.

A soldier was separated from his unit and finally joined the ranks of another army regiment. He immediately asked an officer, "What can I do?"

"Fall in anywhere," the officer replied; "there's good fighting all along the line." That's good advice for the believer with regard to service in the church: "Fall in anywhere, for both inside and outside the walls of the church there is plenty of ministry to do."

I recall as a high school junior I was asked by the church I attended to serve on the Church Preparation Committee, a task that involved converting a school library into a meeting room for Sunday worship and back into a library afterward each week—not a glamorous task, but a necessary one that I could do. Look for assignments at the church that you can do, and volunteer!

Go to Glow

A growing Christian is a glowing Christian. Glowing believers radiate the likeness of Christ in word and deed (Matthew 5:14–16). Others 'take knowledge that they have been with Jesus' (Acts 4:13), and testify "I perceive that this is an holy man of God, which passeth by us continually" (2 Kings 4:9). The ministry of the church enables the Christian to be both "ensamples to all that believe" (1 Thessalonians 1:7) and penetrating lights to those in spiritual darkness (Luke 11:36; Proverbs 4:18; Isaiah 42:6).

Go to Obey and Not to Stray

"You should not stay away from the church meetings, as some are doing, but you should meet together and encourage each other. Do this even more as you see the day coming" (Hebrews 10:25, NCV).

Faithfulness in attendance at church is an act of loving obedience to the Lord Jesus Christ, one which helps insure the believer does not **stray into sin (Hebrews 10:26).**

Go for Accountability

Another powerful reason for church attendance is for accountability to its spiritual leaders (pastor, student minister, and others). "Obey those who rule over you, and be submissive, for they watch out for your souls, as those who must give account. Let them do so with joy and not with grief, for that would be unprofitable for you" (Heb. 13:17 NKJV). Believers are to be submissive to spiritual leaders within the church for they "watch out for your souls," granting protection from heresy while enabling spiritual health. No believer is beyond the need of accountability, and it's neat that God has established ministers in the local church to hold Christians' feet to the fire spiritually when otherwise drifting would occur. Don't forfeit the tremendous help available from spiritual leaders in the church by failure to attend.

In regard to the church, not all are the same. The benchmarks of the type church to attend include its proclamation of the deity, virgin birth, virtuous life, vicarious death, victorious resurrection, verifiable ascension, and visible return to earth of Jesus Christ, coupled with an uncompromising stand on the infallibility of the Bible.

ASK YOURSELF

What is the New Testament Church?

What are the eight reasons cited for its support and attendance?

Have you been guilty of placing greater emphasis on a Christian club on campus than the church?

Are you a member of a church; and, if not, why not?

Comment upon Rich DeVos' statement regarding the importance of community worship with fellow believers.

Why is church involvement superior to that of involvement in a parachurch organization?

Does it matter what type of church one attends?

7   Discovering Your Spiritual Gift

"There are different kinds of gifts, but the same Spirit. There are different kinds of service, but the same Lord."—1 Corinthians 12:4–5.

You may have talent and thought it was a gift—and in a way it is. All talents are given by God. But talents are not unique to the saved—unsaved people have talents, as well. Spiritual gifts, though, are supernatural, grace gifts—not earned or learned.[30]—Adrian Rogers

May I ask you to take a minute to sit quietly and take stock of all that God has given you? I am sure you will put yourself down as being utterly without gifts. Now think of all the abilities you have....What has God trusted you with? Add up each item, and compute the total sum. What talents and gifts has the Lord given you? Remember, of everyone who has been given much, much will be demanded. What, then, has been given to you?[31]—C. H. Spurgeon

"A spiritual gift, quite simply, is a God-given ability for service."[32] Spiritual gifts are "special gifts bestowed by the Holy Spirit upon Christians for the purpose of building up the church."[33] (Nelson's Illustrated Bible Dictionary)

Every believer possesses at least one spiritual gift to utilize in service to the Lord. A spiritual gift is not to be confused with natural talent. Talent is derived from birth from parents, whereas a spiritual gift is received supernaturally from God at conversion. Talents are possessed by non-Christians and Christians; only Christians have spiritual gifts. Talents often are used to benefit oneself; spiritual gifts are to benefit others (1 Corinthians 12:7).

"Spiritual gifts," states Adrian Rogers, "are not toys but tools, not for your enjoyment but for your employment."[34] Gifts are given that believers may glorify God and edify (build up, mature) the Body of Christ (the church).

Talents and gifts must be recognized and developed for maximum potential. Both ought to be used to further God's work, but spiritual gifts specifically are given to this purpose. A person talented to speak, sing, administrate, or lead may excel in using these talents outside the Kingdom realm, but not as effectively within it. In other words, a school teacher will not be as effective teaching Sunday school; a good lecturer will not be as effective preaching; a bank manager will not be as effective as a church administrator. It is the supernaturally gifted who are able to perform spiritual assignments the most effectively. At conversion, God may or may not give a gift or gifts that parallel talents possessed.

John Piper surmises the purpose for spiritual gifts. "The aim of all spiritual gifts is 'that in everything God might be glorified through Jesus Christ' (1 Peter 4:11). This means that God's aim in giving us gifts, and in giving us the faith to exercise them, is that His glory might be displayed. He wants us and the world to marvel at Him and think He is fantastic. The stupendous reality of God is all encompassing. 'For from Him and through Him and to Him are all things' (Romans 11:36). And there is nothing more thrilling, more joyful, more meaningful, more satisfying than to find our niche in the eternal unfolding of God's glory. Our gift may look small, but as a part of the revelation of God's infinite glory, it takes on stupendous proportions."[35]

The number of spiritual gifts varies, according to Bill Bright. He states, "Dr. Charles Caldwell Ryrie, respected scholar and theologian, in his book The Holy Spirit lists 14 spiritual gifts. Dr. Peter Wagner, also a respected scholar and theologian, lists 27 gifts in his book. And most other writers number the gifts somewhere in between."[36] The consensus of theologians is that Paul's listing of gifts in 1 Corinthians 12, Ephesians 4, and Romans 12 is representative, not exhaustive.

Gifts vary in nature and responsibility, but all are vitally important to the operation of the kingdom. Paul writes, "There are diversities of gifts, but the same Spirit. And there are differences of administrations, but the same Lord. And there are diversities of operations, but it is the same God which worketh all in all" (1 Corinthians 12:4–6).

Spiritual Gifts

Matthew Henry: "The greater the gifts are, the more the possessor is exposed to temptations and the larger is the measure of grace needed to keep him humble and spiritual."[37]

Wisdom (1 Corinthians 12:8)—"makes known to the people of the Lord the purpose of God for them in a particular situation (cf. Acts 6:1–7; 15:13–21)."[38] J. Vernon McGee states, "'Wisdom' is insight into the truth of the Word of God."[39] This wisdom is not derived from one's ability to figure out a situation, but it is supernaturally given by God to answer a question or solve a problem.[40]

Knowledge (1 Corinthians 12:8)—John MacArthur states that the gift of knowledge is "the ability to understand and speak God's truth with insight into the mysteries of His Word that cannot be known apart from God's revelation (Rom. 16:25; Eph. 3:3; Col. 1:26; 2:2; 4:3; cf. 1 Cor. 13:2).[41]

Discernment (1 Corinthians 12:10)—to distinguish heresy from truth by judging whether its origination is from God or Satan; sense hypocrisy or dishonesty in others.

Faith (1 Corinthians 12:9)—to trust God completely, to place an unusual reliance upon Him regardless of circumstances; an unshakeable confidence/assurance in God's promises and power to accomplish a matter. The London pastor and orphanage director George Mueller clearly displayed the gift of faith.

Giving (Romans 12:8)—the ability to give money and other forms of wealth cheerfully and generously to enhance the cause of Christ.

Exhortation or Encouragement (Romans 12:8)—to spur another forward in Christ through counsel, comfort, correction, and/or mentoring.

Hospitality (1 Peter 4:9–10)—kindness to believers and strangers in one's home/church with provision of food/shelter.

Serving/Helps (Romans 12:7; 1 Corinthians 12:28; Ephesians 4:12)—Christian service in general; identifying a task small or large that needs to be done in the church/Kingdom and using one's resources to accomplish it. As I stated in the previous chapter, as a high school student I was asked to serve on the Preparation Committee at church, a task that involved setting up chairs prior to worship and taking them down afterward. This task was a gift of ministering.

Mercy (Romans 12:8)—deeds of kindness performed with a cheerful countenance to the sick, persecuted, imprisoned, hurting; ability to shower forgiveness upon the undeserving. "Those who care for people in the hospital, those who sympathize with those going through a traumatic relational experience, or those who cry with those experiencing the heartbreak of divorce have the gift of mercy."[42]

Prophecy (Romans 12:6)—William Barclay states, "It usually has to do with forthtelling the Word of God. The prophet is the man who can announce the Christian message with the authority of one who knows."[43] The apostle Paul defines the purpose of this gift in 1 Corinthians 14:3 in this manner: "But one who prophesies strengthens others, encourages them, and comforts them" (NLT).

Administration (Romans 12:8; I Corinthians 12:28)—to steer the church in the accomplishment of God-given goals and biblical directives through organization, planning and execution.

Ruling (Romans 12:8; 1 Timothy 3:4, 12)—pertains to the government of the local church and the ability to so govern.

Teaching (Romans 12:7; I Corinthians 12:28; Ephesians 4:11)—to instruct others in the Bible in a manner that is understandable and which enhances spiritual growth.

Leadership (Romans 12:8)—ability by example/word to motivate, guide, lead others in the body of Christ to move in a certain direction or to accomplish specific tasks.

Evangelism (Ephesians 4:11)—to be divinely set apart for the work of vocational evangelism. C. Peter Wagoner states that some evangelists have the missionary gift, the ability to minister effectively in other cultures as well as their own, and they should. Evangelists who do not possess the missionary gift should focus on a monocultural [single, nondiverse] ministry.[44]

Pastor/Teacher (Ephesians 4:11)—to be divinely commissioned to be the spiritual shepherd of a church.

Missionary (Ephesians 3:6–8)—spiritual ability and passionate desire to minister among the unsaved in places that are culturally distinct from their own (home or abroad). This is not specifically included in the gifts' lists, but it is seemingly indicated in Ephesians 3:6–8.

Identifying Gifts

Some erroneously think they possess a certain gift, and others are unaware of their spiritual gift. Warren Wiersbe addresses this problem: "It is not wrong for a Christian to recognize gifts in his own life and in the lives of others. What is wrong is the tendency to have a false evaluation of ourselves. Nothing causes more damage in a local church than a believer who overrates himself and tries to perform a ministry that he cannot do. (Sometimes the opposite is true, and people undervalue themselves. Both attitudes are wrong.)"[45]

In *The Canvas Cathedral*, Lewis Drummond shares the five ways Billy Graham encourages believers to discover their giftedness.

(1) Realize they do have at least one spiritual gift. Some may well have more, but all have at least one.

(2) Pray to discover spiritual giftedness.

(3) Be willing to use spiritual gifts to bring honor to Christ and the blessings of the Lord to the church.

(4) Explore what the Bible says about the spiritual gifts, searching out examples of how they are employed.

(5) Acquire a knowledge of their own self and abilities.

Finding out may be a lengthy process, but it is the basis for any believer's service to the church. It is also crucial to recognize that all gifts are necessary and none are inherently better than others.[46]

You can discover your gift(s) in service. By doing Christian work, giftedness is often revealed. Spiritual believers also may be of help in identifying giftedness. It is imperative to identify your gift(s) and operate within its/their confines for maximum effectiveness in ministry.

Bill Gothard uses a word picture to help believers understand their possible gifts. A family of seven, each representing a spiritual gift are enjoying dinner together. The lady serving the dessert trips over a fire truck and falls to the floor, along with the dessert. It made a huge mess! Pecan pie was mixed with chocolate pie, and coconut cake was splattered on the floor. Mentally, as you picture this, what would have been your immediate reaction?

Based on your gift, this may be what you said.

Prophecy—"That's what happens when you're not careful!" And then a follow-up—"People should not leave their toys in the doorway!"

Serving—"Oh, let me help you clean it up."

Teaching—"The reason she tripped is that there was a toy fire truck left in the doorway, and she did not see it.

Exhortation—"Next time, let's make sure there are no toys in the doorway and that we watch where we are going. We can learn from this and be better because of it."

Giving—"I'll be happy to buy a new dessert."

Administration—"Jim, would you get the mop. Sue, please help pick it up. And, Mary, help me fix some other dessert. Theresa, see if our server is okay."

Mercy—"Don't feel badly. It could have happened to anyone."[47]

After going through these descriptions, which can you identify with?

Elmer Towns gives this advice for when you are endeavoring to discover your giftedness: "Don't wait to perform a ministry because you are not sure it doesn't match your giftedness. There's no verse in the Bible that tells you to do that. As a matter of fact, the opposite is taught: 'And whatsoever ye do, do it heartily, as to the Lord, and not unto men' (Colossians 3:23). So, begin now doing the ministry that's close at hand and needs doing."[48] Regardless of the spiritual gift(s) believers possess, all are spiritually responsible to exalt the Savior (by devotion, holiness, and obedience), edify the saints (building one another up), and evangelize the lost (reaching the unreached with the Gospel).

If knowledgeable of your spiritual gift(s), are you presently using them as God intended; or, as with Timothy's, do they need fanning into full flame (2 Timothy 1:6)? C. H. Spurgeon states, "The gifts and graces of Christians are like a coal fire which frequently requires stirring and fanning as well as feeding with fuel. There are times with us when we become dull and heavy, doing little or nothing—restless, indifferent—and then it is that we require rebuking. If there is a solid foundation of real grace in us, we only need to be fanned into flame, and right away the fire begins to burn."[49]

ASK YOURSELF

Contrast the difference between a talent and a spiritual gift.

Is it permissible for a believer to seek a specific gift of personal preference?

Are spiritual gifts for one's own benefit or that of another?

How can you know what gift(s) you possess?

What gift(s) do you know you possess, and what gift(s) might you possibly possess?

Explain why a person who is greatly talented may not be divinely gifted in the same element.

Discuss this truth: Talents as well as spiritual gifts are given from God and should be used for His glory.

Explain the meaning of 1 Corinthians 12:15.

Visit www.elmertowns.com to take a spiritual gift test. It will automatically give you a profile of your spiritual gifts.

8   The Agonizing Doubt of Salvation

"Examine yourselves to see if your faith is genuine. Test yourselves."—2 Corinthians 13:5 (NLT)

My conscience hath a thousand several tongues, and every tongue brings in a several tale, and every tale condemns me for a villain.[50]—William Shakespeare

So here we are in Christ, who is God; and no burglar, not even Satan himself, can separate us from the love of God in Christ Jesus (Rom. 8:31–39).[51]—A.T. Robertson

Doubt regarding one's salvation can be most agonizing and stressing. It robs one of peace and impacts his or her service. It could be easily put to rest if only its source were known. But that is the basic problem, isn't it? Is the doubt from God to reveal counterfeit salvation, or is it of Satan to disturb fellowship with God? To believers with firm assurance of salvation, this confusing issue may be seen as a no-brainer to solve, but not so for those who wrestle intensely with it to the point of wits' end. Among doubters are God-fearing people who attest that at some point they invited Jesus into their heart and later became baptized members of a church.

"There are two extremes to be avoided," writes John MacArthur, "in the matter of assurance. One is the error of settling for an assurance that comes too easily. This can lead to a shallow, false assurance and a fatal spiritual apathy. This false assurance is the bane of our age. At the other extreme is a chronic uncertainty that leads to a preoccupation with oneself, one's fears, and one's failings. It results in a vacillating, feeble faith."[52]

All who counsel doubters must be careful not to give false hope to those who have no hope while affirming hope to those who possess true salvation. "If a person is wrong about being right with God," states Donald Whitney, "[then] ultimately it doesn't matter what else he or she is right about."[53]

The assurance of salvation is "the birthright and privilege of every true believer in Christ."[54] This assurance is not only possible, but it is part and parcel of the normal Christian life. Of a certainty, God desires all His children to be confident of their place in His family. The apostle John echoes this emphatic fact. "These things have I written unto you that believe on the name of the Son of God; that ye may know that ye have eternal life" (1 John 5:13). The moment one repents and in faith receives Jesus Christ as Lord and Savior, his or her name is written in permanent ink in the Lamb's Book of Life in Heaven. Clearly, one's salvation is not to be a hope-so, think-so, gambling-so, or perhaps-so knowledge, but an unequivocal know-so reality. John Stott well stated, "Clearly one cannot enjoy a gift unless one knows that one possesses it. Therefore, if God means us to receive and enjoy eternal life, He must mean us to know we possess it."[55] No one desires more than I do that doubting Christians become shouting Christians.

Salvation doubt can be traced to one or more of seven things: (1) doubt that God kept His promise to save; (2) doubt that the condition of salvation was understood; (3) doubt that the heart was sincere in what was done; (4) doubt that once one is saved, he is always saved; (5) doubt based on feeling or not feeling a certain way; (6) doubt based on sinful conduct; (7) doubt that the real thing was received.

To personalize these factors of doubt, the doubter needs to ask these questions. Do I absolutely believe God will keep His Word and save all who call upon Him in faith and repentance? Did I understand when I prayed the sinner's prayer that I was a guilty sinner separated from God and that Jesus' death on Calvary made it possible to acquire forgiveness and reconciliation to God through faith and repentance (Acts 20:21)? Was I in earnest, sincere in praying the sinner's prayer? Though it is contrary to the teaching of Scripture, do I believe that it is possible for a person to lose salvation if he falters in sin? Was I expecting a certain type of emotional encounter that did not occur? Has there been a change in my conduct and convictions? Do I doubt that I got the real deal?

Obviously, the answers to these questions cast light on whether or not one is in possession of eternal life. If a person doubts understanding the need (Romans 3:23) and/or means of salvation (Acts 20:21) or sincerity in praying the sinner's prayer (2 Corinthians 7:10) or has not evidenced a change in lifestyle, then he failed to get the real thing (2 Corinthians 5:17). Jesus forewarned of such a possibility when He said, "Many will say to me in that day, Lord, Lord, have we not prophesied in thy name? and in thy name have cast out devils? and in thy name done many wonderful works? And then will I profess unto them, I never knew you: depart from me, ye that work iniquity" (Matthew 7:22–23). This knowledge should clear the doubt revealing the need to be genuinely saved immediately.

Doubt that arises from distrust that God saves all who call upon Him in faith and repentance, doubt that salvation is permanent, or an expectation of a "rush" at the time of salvation or afterward reveals ignorance of biblical teaching which can easily be resolved by three things: God's Word *to* you, God's work *for* you, and God's witness *in* you.

God's Word to You. "These things have I written unto you that believe on the name of the Son of God; that ye may know that ye have eternal life, and that ye may believe on the name of the Son of God" (1 John 5:13). Unlike John's Gospel that is written specifically to win the lost, the Epistle of First John is written to saints to assure them of eternal life based on the promises of the Word of God. Study it thoroughly, and it will reveal the genuineness

47

of salvation. The bottom line concerning salvation is what God says in Holy Scripture (Romans 10:9–13; John 3:16; Acts 20:21). "He is the Great Physician and will heal our souls instantly if we will trust Him. As we would trust a doctor and submit to his treatment and depend on him for results, so we should trust Jesus today regarding our souls."[56]

God's Work for You. Jesus died on the Cross and was raised from the dead to make salvation possible. The instant a person invites Christ into his or her life (through repentance and faith), Jesus' work of reconciliation and regeneration occurs. Whereas sincerity of heart must accompany salvation, feelings may or may not. No one is saved, nor is assurance of it gained, for feeling a certain way. Feelings are not proof of salvation. A person is not to *feel* salvation, but *"faith"* salvation. The proof of salvation rests upon God's Word. While the believer certainly should feel relief that things are eternally settled with God and should feel awesome gratitude to God, validating salvation by emotional experiences is not biblical (Romans 8:16). Fact, faith, and feeling are like a steam locomotive train. Fact is the engine that pulls the train, faith is the boiler that fuels the engine, and feeling is the caboose. The train must have an engine and a boiler to function, but the caboose is optional.

"And therefore it was imputed to him for righteousness. Now it was not written for his sake alone, that it was imputed to him; But for us also, to whom it shall be imputed, if we believe on him that raised up Jesus our Lord from the dead" (Romans 4:22–24). Abraham wasn't saved by his own merit or good works, but rather by Christ's righteousness which was imputed to him by God.

The word *impute* means "to attribute to another, to pass to one's account." In pointing out the futility of self-righteousness and the must of divine imputation of Christ's righteousness as a means of salvation, the apostle Paul declared, "That I may gain Christ, and may be found in Him, not having a righteousness of my own derived from the Law, but that which is through faith in Christ, the righteousness which comes from God on the basis of faith" (Philippians 3:8–9 ASV). Paul says a person must have the righteousness of God that comes by faith in Christ in order to enter Heaven. At the moment of salvation, God covers a person with the canopy of Christ's perfected righteousness (imputes); and from that moment forward, when He looks at that person, He sees Christ's righteousness (2 Corinthians 5:21), not any righteousness that the person might claim. We refer to this as the judicial forgiveness of God. What an awesome and glorious truth!

The apostle Paul gives yet another beautiful picture of judicial forgiveness when he says, "When you were spiritually dead because of your sins and because you were not free from the power of your sinful self, God made you alive with Christ, and he forgave all our sins. He canceled the debt, which listed all the rules we failed to follow. He took away that record with its rules and nailed it to the cross" (Colossians 2:13–14 NCV).

In ancient days, a list of the crime(s) of the executed were hung on the cross with them. God took every sin we would ever commit and nailed it to Jesus' cross. Jesus paid the full payment for our sin so that we might be reconciled to God. The Christian is no longer in bondage to the debt of sin (its penalty), because Jesus paid it once and for all. "Jesus paid it all; all to Him I owe. Sin had left a crimsoned stain. He washed it white as snow."

C. H. Spurgeon explains why some believers doubt their salvation. "Some Christians seem to be accepted in their own experience; at least, that is their apprehension. When their spirit is lively and their hopes bright, they think God accepts them, for they feel so high, so heavenly-minded, so drawn above the earth! But when their souls cleave to the dust, they are the victims of the fear that they are no longer accepted. If they could but see that all their high joys do not exalt them and all their low despondencies do not really depress them in their Father's sight, but that they stand accepted in One who never alters, in One who is always the beloved of God, always perfect, always without spot or wrinkle, or any such thing, how much happier they would be, and how much more they would honour the Saviour! Rejoice then, believer, in this: thou art accepted 'in the beloved' (Ephesians 1:6). Thy sins trouble thee; but God has cast thy sins behind his back, and thou art accepted in the Righteous One. Thou hast to fight with corruption and to wrestle with temptation, but thou art already accepted in Him who has overcome the powers of evil. The Devil tempts thee. Be of good cheer; he cannot destroy thee, for thou art accepted in Him who has broken Satan's head. Know by full assurance thy glorious standing. Even glorified souls are not more accepted than thou art. They are only accepted in heaven 'in the beloved,' and thou art even now accepted in Christ after the same manner."[57]

These Scripture texts reveal Christ's work in the life of the sinner regarding sins at the *very moment* of salvation:

- He takes them away (John 1:29);
- He forgets them (Hebrews 10:17);
- He washes them away (Isaiah 1:17–18);
- He blots them out (Isaiah 43:25);
- He wipes them out like a cloud (Isaiah 44:22);
- He pardons them (Isaiah 55:7);
- He buries them in the depths of the sea (Micah 7:19);
- He separates them from the sinner as far as the east is from the west (Psalm 103:12).

The Old Testament provides a remarkable illustration of the work of Christ. In Israel on the Day of Atonement, the high priest placed his hands upon the head of a flawless goat and confessed the sins of the people, symbolically transferring their sin to the goat. This "scapegoat"—sin-bearer—of the people was led into a remote part of the desert and let loose where it would never be found (Leviticus 16:20–22). This Old Testament scapegoat expresses New Testament atonement. Jesus Christ is the Supreme Scapegoat,

50

provided by God to forgive sin and bear it into the "desert" of everlasting forgetfulness.

God's Witness in Me. There are two ways God gives witness to His presence in the believer.

(1) The witness of the Holy Spirit. At conversion, the Holy Spirit takes up residence in the believer's heart and assures the believer that he or she has passed from death to life. "The Spirit itself beareth witness with our spirit, that we are the children of God" (Romans 8:16).

"The Holy Spirit," states C. H. Spurgeon, "is often pleased, in a most gracious manner, to witness with our spirits of the love of Jesus. He takes of the things of Christ and reveals them unto us. No voice is heard from the clouds, and no vision is seen in the night, but we have a testimony more sure than either of these. If an angel should fly from Heaven and inform the saint personally of the Savior's love to him, the evidence would not be one whit more satisfactory than that which is borne in the heart by the Holy Ghost."[58]

Jason Gray, in the song "Remind Me Who I Am," identifies with the believer who struggles with assurance, petitioning a loving God to help him know he is indeed saved.

Tell me once again who I am to You, who I am to You;
Tell me, lest I forget who I am to You, that I belong to You, to You.[59]

According to Romans 8:16, such a heartfelt prayer will not go unanswered, for God will grant confirmation by the Holy Spirit's witness in the believer.

(2) The witness of a changed life. Conversion results in change (2 Corinthians 5:17). It is impossible for a born-again believer to remain the same in conscience, conviction, and conduct. The way a person views these things changes. An old African-American saying makes this point. "The day I got saved, my feet got a brand new walk, and my speech got a brand new talk." A difference occurs at salvation that continues to progress throughout a Christian's life.

"Is Jesus Christ," asks Adrian Rogers, "the Lord of your life? Jesus said, 'Why call ye me, Lord, Lord, and do not the things which I say?' (Luke 6:46). Here's a riddle I want to solve for you. On the one hand, the Bible says that we know that we're saved because we keep His commandments (1 John 2:3). On the other hand, the Bible teaches us that it is possible to sin (1 John 1:8–9). The key word is 'keep.' It is the same word used years ago by sailors who navigated by the stars at night. A sailor's goal was to keep the stars. As a child of God, His commandments are the stars by which you navigate your life. Is keeping His commandments the burning desire of your heart? It is, if you've met the Christ of Calvary."[60]

It's time for the doubter to have inner peace, not stress; joy, not despair; and freedom, not bondage. It's time the battle of the mind and soul caused by doubt ended. It's time for Satan once and for all to be driven back. It's time that haunting and agonizing doubt cease to plague forever. To gain this deliverance, the doubter must do one of two things.

First, trust God that He in fact did what was promised when the conditions of salvation were met (new birth). "Whenever our conscience condemns us, we will be reassured that God is greater than our conscience and knows everything" (1 John 3:20, GWT). Satan attacked the Word of God in tempting Eve, saying to her that what God said wasn't really what He meant. She believed Satan's lie over God's Truth. The shield of protection came down, and sin entered the world (Genesis 3:1–6). Satan yet toys with the minds of

God's children, seeking to have them believe that God really did not mean what He promised about salvation. Believe God over the accusing doubt Satan has sown in the mind.

Upon Satan's thrust of the fiery dart of doubt to the soul, the saint must offensively use God's Word to drive him back. I suggest writing on an index card several key Bible verses that specifically relate to assurance of salvation which can be voiced to Satan upon attack (1 John 5:11–13; 2 Corinthians 10:5; Romans 10:13; John 3:17–18; 1 John 4:13–15). J. W. Alexander said, "Those who have had the most abiding assurance of God's love are those who have been most in meditation on the written assurances of that love."[61]

Second, admit the conditions of salvation were not understood and/or sincerity of heart was not exhibited (counterfeit salvation) and accept Jesus Christ based upon new understanding with sincerity as Lord and Savior (Romans 10:13). The doubter must say no to a former religious experience in order to say yes to authentic salvation.

Get the doubt resolved now

The great British Baptist preacher of the nineteenth century, C. H. Spurgeon, is renown among ministers worldwide. Spurgeon became pastor of the New Park Street Chapel in London at the age of twenty, drawing crowds of thousands each Sunday and moving into the Metropolitan Tabernacle just seven years later. This preacher has more books in print than any other minister, past or present. Yet this great spiritual giant had his battles with salvation doubt.[62]

Listen carefully to Spurgeon's challenge regarding doubt in his sermon *Assurance Sought.*

"I can understand a man doubting whether he is truly converted or not, but I cannot countenance his apathy in resting quiet till he has solved the riddle. You may say, "Tis a point I long to

53

know.' But, oh, Beloved, how can you trifle; how can you give sleep to your eyes till you have known it? Not know whether you are in Christ or not? Perhaps unreconciled, perhaps already condemned, perhaps upon the brink of Hell, perhaps with nothing more to keep you out of [Hell] than the breath that is in your nostrils or the circulating drop of blood which any one of ten thousand haps or mishaps may stop, and then your career is closed—your life story ended! What? Sit on such a volcano, take it easy on the brink of such a precipice and content yourself with merely saying, 'I am but a doubting one'? I entreat you; I beseech you; shake off this sluggishness! Ask the Lord to say unto your soul tonight, 'I am your salvation.' He is able and He is willing! You know that, Beloved. He will do it for you when you eagerly seek it from Him."[63]

Oh, how well do I remember
How I doubted day by day,
For I did not know for certain
That my sins were washed away.
When the Spirit tried to tell me,
I would not the truth receive;
I endeavored to be happy
And to make myself believe.

When the truth came close and searching,
All my joys would disappear,
For I did not have the witness
Of the Spirit bright and clear.
If at times the coming judgment
Would appear before my mind,
Oh, it made me so uneasy,
For God's smile I could not find.

When the Lord sent faithful servants
Who would dare to preach the truth,
How my heart did so condemn me
As the Spirit gave reproof!
Satan said at once, "'Twill ruin
You to now confess your state;
Keep on working and professing,
And you'll enter Heaven's gate."

But at last I tired of living
Such a life of fear and doubt,
For I wanted God to give me
Something I would know about,
So the truth would make me happy
And the light would clearly shine;
And the Spirit gave assurance
That I'm His and He is mine.

So I prayed to God in earnest
And not caring what folks said.
I was hungry for the blessing;
My pour soul—it must be fed.
Then at last by faith I touched Him;
And, like sparks from smitten steel,
Just so quick salvation reached me.
Oh, bless God, I know it's real!

But it's real; it's real;
Oh, I know it's real!
Praise God, the doubts are settled,
For I know, I know it's real.[64]

"To say, 'I hope so; I trust so' is comfortable," states Spurgeon, "and there are thousands in the fold of Jesus who hardly ever get much further. But to reach the essence of consolation, you must say, 'I know.' Ifs, buts, and perhapses are sure murderers of peace and comfort. Doubts are dreary things in times of sorrow. Like wasps they sting the soul! If I have any suspicion that Christ is not mine, then there is vinegar mingled with the gall of death; but if I know that Jesus lives for me, then darkness is not dark. Even the night is light about me."[65]

Don't be content with a "hope-so" salvation. Rest not until you honestly can say, "Blessed assurance, Jesus is mine" and the "thousand several tongues" that condemn are silenced.

ASK YOURSELF

Do you possess doubt regarding salvation? If so, which of the seven causes or combination of causes for doubt is responsible?

Is the source of the doubt from God or Satan, and cite how you know?

What role does feeling play in salvation?

How can one who passes the "test" of being saved repel the fiery darts of doubt that Satan hurls upon the mind?

Read back through the hymn "It's Real." In relation to the stanzas of this hymn, where are you in the quest for assurance? Stanza one: eaten up with plaguing doubt; stanzas two and three: miserable and stressed; stanza four: desperate for resolve; stanza five: receptive to the truth, or stanza six: certain of salvation beyond all doubt.

At what stanza do you long to live?

If you are satisfied that you are at stanza two, then move to stanza five this moment by inviting Christ into your life as Lord and Savior.

9   Staying Clean in an Unclean World

"Blessed are the pure in heart: for they shall see God."—
Matthew 5:8.

My enemy is within the citadel. Come with almighty power
and cast him out, pierce him to death, and abolish in me every
particle of carnal life this day.[66]—Puritan Prayer

In New Testament times, the Greeks used "purity" to refer
to something physically clean, like a cloth free of dirt. To them,
something was pure when it was free from additives, things that
would hinder it from being used for its designed purpose. A
substance that was contaminated could be free to do its intended
work once the interference was removed. For example, a surgical
cloth was pure when separated from deadly bacteria.

You are pure in heart when the sinful additives are
removed, allowing life to be lived as God designed it to be lived. At
the core of the meaning of heart purity is right motives in doing
right, for wrong motives equally contaminate the heart. Based upon
this definition, the beatitude may be rendered, 'Blessed is the man
whose conduct and motive in thought and deed is unmixed with the
contaminating agents of this world, for he shall see God.'

The Apostle Paul put it in this fashion, "But among you
there must *not be even a hint* of sexual immorality, or of any kind of
impurity, or of greed, because these are improper for God's holy
people." (Ephesians 5:3, NIV, italics added). It is impossible to see
God through heart lenses that are contaminated with sin.

The promise to the pure in heart is that "they shall see
God." A person sees only what he is able to see. Two men view

paintings in a famous art museum. One is an art connoisseur; the other is not. The art connoisseur sees priceless art, while the other fails to see any worth in the same paintings. One can only see what he *can* see. The unclean heart cannot clearly see God, know God, nor serve God successfully.

In contrast, the clean heart presently sees God clearly and will have no trouble recognizing Him upon His return. Take a moment and pray with the psalmist, "Search me, O God, and know my heart: try me, and know my thoughts: And see if there be any wicked way in me, and lead me in the way everlasting" (Psalm 139:23-24). Gold is pure when it has been separated by the refiner's fire from all foreign matter. The same is true for the heart.

ASK YOURSELF

Is your heart pure?

What contaminating additives might be interfering with God's purpose being fulfilled with your life?

Might the difficulty you experience in knowing God's will lie in the fact that you cannot see Him due to foggy heart lenses?

Explain the meaning of the words "not even a hint."

10   Plug into the Power Source

"Be not drunk with wine, wherein is excess; but be filled with the Spirit."—Ephesians 5:18.

It said that the average Christian and the average church are somewhere bogged down between Calvary and Pentecost. They have been to Calvary for pardon, but they have not been to Pentecost for power. Bethlehem means God *with* us; Calvary means God *for* us; but Pentecost means God *in* us.[67]—Jerry Vines

A slow-witted farmer purchased a chainsaw after being told that it was guaranteed to cut down forty trees a day. In a week's time, he returned the chainsaw to the store. The salesman inquired as to the problem, and the farmer replied, "I have been working my head off, and I ain't able ta bring down more than five trees a day." The salesman, with a frown, looked at the chainsaw and then pulled its starter cord. As it roared to life, the farmer jumped back and exclaimed, "What's that noise?"

Sadly, far too many believers, when told about the liberating, illuminating, triumphing, enabling, equipping, and emboldening power of the Holy Spirit available to them so they can live the victorious Christian life, exclaim, "What's that?" Such ignorance leads to a life of religious self-effort, which results in defeat, discouragement, and little fruit. Christians who are not walking under the control of the Holy Spirit are like the slow-witted farmer; they are trying to cut down trees with a chainsaw that's not powered on.

There is but one baptism of the Holy Spirit, and that occurs at conversion, but there can and should be many infillings of the Holy Spirit throughout the Christian's life (Ephesians 5:18). The

Baptism of the Holy Spirit is when the Holy Spirit takes up residence in the Christian at salvation; the infilling of the Holy Spirit is when the Christian yields to the Spirit's control, allowing Him not only to be resident but also President in his life (Galatians 5:16; 25). It is only when the believer relinquishes control of his life to the Holy Spirit's dominion that His power is fully tapped.

How, then, can a person be infilled with the Holy Spirit?

1. It takes a desire to be under His constant control (John 7:37–39). The Holy Spirit only infills the person who has nothing less than an aching void for more of His fullness and power.

2. It takes confession of sin (1 John 1:7–9). Identify, renounce, and repent of the sin in your life. Present yourself as a clean vessel for the Holy Spirit to infill and use.

3. Next, make a presentation of the total self to God (Romans 12:1–2), holding nothing back.

4. In faith, claim the promise of the infilling of the Holy Spirit. God commanded: "And do not get drunk with wine...but be filled with the Spirit" (Ephesians 5:18 ESV). Based upon God's command to be infilled, walk in faith, believing the promise that all who meet the condition of the command are infilled. "You fathers—if your children ask for a fish, do you give them a snake instead? Or if they ask for an egg, do you give them a scorpion? Of course not! So if you sinful people know how to give good gifts to your children, how much more will your heavenly Father give the Holy Spirit to those who ask him" (Luke 11:11–13 NLT).

How to pray in faith to be infilled with the Holy Spirit.

Heavenly Father, I am sorry for usurping Your authority to alone order my steps. Please forgive me of this sin and take Thy rightful place upon my heart's throne as Lord. I now submit myself in totality unto Your control. I do pray for the infilling of the Holy Spirit as commanded, and do claim that infilling based upon faith according to Your promise. Thank you, Lord, for now taking charge of my life completely and for providing the power necessary to live victoriously and abundantly. In Jesus' name I pray. Amen.

ASK YOURSELF

How is the slow-witted farmer who failed to pull the cord of the chainsaw like the Christian who seeks to live victoriously for Christ without being infilled with the Holy Spirit?

At this moment, is the Holy Spirit President in your life?

If not, what do you need to do to allow Him to be so?

How different might your life be if it were lived in His power instead of your own?

11 Practical Disciplines for Claiming Victory over Satan

"Stay alert! Watch out for your great enemy, the devil. He prowls around like a roaring lion, looking for someone to devour."— I Peter 5:8 NLT

What with pitfalls and snares, weak knees, weary feet, and subtle enemies, no child of God would stand fast for an hour, were it not for the faithful love [Christ] which will not suffer his foot to be moved.[68]—C. H. Spurgeon

Sin wants to remain unknown. It shuns the light. In the darkness of the unexpressed, it poisons the whole being of a person. This can happen even in the midst of a pious community. In confession, the light of the Gospel breaks into the darkness and seclusion of the heart. The sin must be brought into the light. The unexpressed must be openly spoken and acknowledged. All that is secret and hidden is made manifest. It is a struggle until the sin is openly admitted, but God breaks gates of brass and bars of iron (Psalm 107:16). The sinner surrenders; he gives up all his evil. He gives his heart to God, and he finds the forgiveness of all his sin in the fellowship of Jesus Christ and his brother. The expressed, acknowledged sin has lost all its power.[69]—Dietrich Bonhoeffer

An apartment renter is harassed by the landlord of the complex continuously. The landlord never allows the renter a moment of peace but is always on his case about something— keeping his apartment clean or repairing items he didn't break or demanding rent before it is due. In time, the complex is sold, and a new landlord, totally opposite of the former, is hired. It is hog heaven for the renter.

The renter one night is surprised when he opens the door to the strenuous knocking of the former landlord who is demanding early rent and certain repairs. What is he to do? Is he to slug it out with him? Is he to do as he asks? No, regardless of the man's threats or the shaking of legal papers in his face, all he has to do is to tell him to take the matter up with his new landlord.

The Christian must respond similarly when his former landlord (Satan) comes knocking at the door with a variety of demands, accusations, and temptations. He must boldly, frankly say, "Take the matter up with my new landlord (Jesus). That's the end of the matter as far as I am concerned." The believer is no longer under the authority of his former landlord, but completely under that of Jesus Christ.

A little girl was once asked, "If Satan were to come to your house and knock at your door, what would you do?"

She answered, "I would not open the door myself. When Satan knocks at my door, I will send the Lord Jesus to the door, and when the Devil sees Him, he will run away! Jesus is my Savior and the One who protects me." Every believer must treat Satan in the same manner.

C. H. Spurgeon, the great London pastor of the nineteenth century, offers great counsel regarding battling Satan when he states, "Thou wast once a servant of Satan, and no king will willingly lose his subjects. Dost thou think that Satan will let thee alone? No, he will be always at thee, for he 'goeth about like a roaring lion, seeking whom he may devour.' Expect trouble, therefore, Christian, when thou lookest beneath thee. Then look around thee. Where art thou? Thou art in an enemy's country, a stranger and a sojourner. The world is not thy friend. If it be, then thou art not God's friend, for he who is the friend of the world is the enemy of God. Be assured that thou shalt find foe-men everywhere. When thou sleepest, think that thou art resting on the battlefield; when thou walkest, suspect an ambush in every hedge."[70]

As in any war, soldiers need a battle plan. I've outlined below the Christian's plan for victory in the fight with Satan.

• Know your enemy and vulnerability. Satan cunningly plots the believer's downfall. His intent is to drag the new believer back down into the mire of sin from which he or she was rescued. Scripture cautions us—by admonition and by example—not to underestimate our enemy's power to bring a Christian down. If the adversary can destroy a Samson, a David, and a Demas, any one of us are vulnerable (Judges 16:18–21; 2 Samuel 11:3–5; 2 Timothy 4:10). Paul cautions, "Let him that thinketh he standeth take heed lest he fall" (1 Corinthians 10:12). And Peter warns, "Be sober, be vigilant; because your adversary the devil, as a roaring lion, walketh about, seeking whom he may devour" (1 Peter 5:8).

• Feed on the Scripture regularly. The intake of megadoses of God's Word builds spiritual muscle to resist the wiles of the devil (Hebrews 4:12).

• Memorize Scripture. David testifies, "Thy word have I hid in mine heart, that I might not sin against thee" (Psalm 119:11). Scripture was the weapon Jesus used to defeat Satan in the wilderness and will likewise be yours. Start memorizing verses that specifically address areas of greatest vulnerability.

• Engage in persistent and passionate prayer. Prayer links you to the Divine power needed to thwart the attack of the enemy (Luke 18:1).

• Enlist a fellow believer to hold you accountable.

• Rely upon the super-duper-natural strength of Jesus Christ to drive Satan and the demons back (Philippians 4:13).

• Maintain intimate communion and fellowship with Christ (Philippians 3:7–11).

• Avoid people, places, and pleasures that present a temptation. Don't give Satan a beachhead into your heart (Ephesians 4:27).

• Attend church faithfully (Hebrews 10:25).

• When you are knocked down, don't stay down. Get up immediately. Don't give Satan the satisfaction of gloating over your sin any longer than it takes to confess it to Christ and get it forgiven (1 John 1:9)! Having confessed the sin, reject Satan's harassment regarding it and press forward.

Amidst a thousand snares I stand
Upheld and guarded by thy hand;
That hand unseen shall hold me still
And lead me to thy holy hill.[71]

ASK YOURSELF

Contrast your former landlord (Satan) with your new one (Jesus).

In what ways does the former landlord seek to harass and depress?

Describe how much better it is to live under "New Management?"

What is Satan's primary intent toward believers?

What nine disciplines help assure victory over Satan?

What does Ephesians 4:27 mean, and how can it be applied to your life?

What is the biblical response to Satan when he harasses you regarding weaknesses and failures? (2 Corinthians 5:21; 1 John 1:7)

What is Satan's greatest weapon against you, and how can it be thwarted?

12   Dressing for Battle

"Put on the whole armour of God, that ye may be able to stand against the wiles of the devil."—Ephesians 6:11.

Satan has, in fact, a plan against the saints of the Most High, which is to wear them out. What is meant by this phrase, "wear out"? It has in it the idea of reducing a little this minute, then reducing a little further the next minute. Reduce a little today; reduce a little tomorrow. Thus the wearing out is almost imperceptible; nevertheless, it is a reducing. The wearing down is scarcely an activity of which one is conscious, yet the end result is that there is nothing left. He will take away your prayer life little by little, and cause you to trust God less and less and yourself more and more, a little at a time. He will make you feel somewhat cleverer than before. Step by step, you are misled to rely more on your own gift, and step by step your heart is enticed away from the Lord. Now, were Satan to strike the children of God with great force at one time, they would know exactly how to resist the enemy, since they would immediately recognize his work. He uses the method of gradualism to wear down the people of God.[72]— Watchman Nee

How can a Christian overcome the tactics of Satan and this "wearing us down" little by little? Ephesians 6:11–18 teaches us that wearing the right protection is the answer.

As a baseball catcher, I wore "armor" that consisted of a chest protector, shin guards, mask, and a glove. This protection kept me from serious injury so I could stay in the game. Just as athletes need protection in the games they play, Ephesians 6 says believers need spiritual armor to protect them in the game of life.

The Belt of Truth

The belt reinforces the believer's need to live his belief. To do that, Christians daily study the Bible and try to live what it teaches. This Belt of Truth holds other pieces of the armor together, giving the soldier freedom of movement. The Belt of Truth holds the believer's life together when things shatter and crumble around him or her and Satan tries to restrict a Christian's freedom to press onward.

The Breastplate of Righteousness

The breastplate reflects the believer's need to start each day clean and holy. The believer's first act of business each morning is to get right before God. No Christian should carry soiled laundry (sin) into a new day, but start fresh and pure.

The Gospel Shoes

Shoes demonstrate the believer's assurance of salvation and his or her willingness to plunge into whatever duty is required. It is important that Christian soldiers walk in full confidence of salvation so that in the time of doubt or temptation they will not stumble and fall. Confidence of salvation enables a life of peace in every circumstance of life, whether good or bad. Gospel shoes also remind saints of the need to share the Good News of the Gospel with the unsaved.

Jon Courson comments, "Having my feet shod with the Gospel of peace means I don't *walk on* people, but I get to *share with* people. The word *Gospel* means "good news." Therefore, as I walk through my day, it is my privilege to say to those in my path, "Good news! The Lord loves you. He knows what you're going through. He can set you free."[73]

The Shield of Faith

The shield speaks of the believer's need to continuously believe God. Genesis 3 records Satan's lie to Eve: "You won't die!"

the serpent hissed. "God knows that your eyes will be opened as soon as you eat it, and you will be like God, knowing both good and evil." The woman was convinced. The fruit looked so fresh and delicious, and it would make her so wise! So she ate some of the fruit (Genesis 3:4–6 NLT). The root cause of Eve's trouble is that she believed Satan over God. Her shield came down, and sin entered the world. Don't be like Eve—always believe God. Every Roman soldier was responsible for providing some measure of protection for comrades in battle, so he carried the shield on his left arm so it protected two-thirds of his own body and one third of the body of the solider on his left. Likewise, Christians are to protect each other by exhibiting faith. This not only serves the one who demonstrates faith, but also encourages other Christian soldiers who come alongside them.

The Helmet of Salvation

The helmet shows the need to look at the finish line in Heaven. The Helmet of Salvation reminds believers there is a finish line ahead where Jesus waits for the saved. This part of the armor assures the believer of salvation and that one day he or she will be in the eternal presence of the King of Kings. This helmet also protects the believer's mind from being dominated by carnal and sensual thoughts.

The Sword of the Spirit

The sword represents the power of Holy Scripture in the believer's life. In His wilderness temptations, Jesus used the Sword of the Spirit (the Word of God) to drive back Satan, declaring, "It is written..." (Matthew 4:1–11). "It is written" is a dagger to Satan's heart. During temptation, believers should quote Scripture that forces Satan to flee—hence, the importance of Scripture memorization (Psalm 119:11).

Two types of swords are mentioned in the Bible. The first was forty inches or more long, requiring the use of two hands to wield it. This sword was used when precision assault was not necessary. The second sword's length ranged from 6 to 18 inches and was easily used in combat in making piercing precise thrusts. It is this sword to which Paul refers in Ephesians 6:17. The lesson here is that when we are battling Satan or his demonic hosts, we can't simply wave the Bible (the large Sword) in his face, thinking that will provide protection. Rather, we must use the small dagger—Scripture that specifically addresses the particular temptation.[74] In order to do this, one obviously must know the Bible well enough to be versed in knowing what texts fit the situation.

The Knees of Prayer

"Praying always with all prayer and supplication in the Spirit, and watching thereunto with all perseverance (Ephesians 6:18) is Paul's final direction in this passage about Christian armor. It is a reminder that success in spiritual battle is simply not possible apart from the divinely infused strength gained through prayer.

The preacher George Allen Smith once stood on a precipice in the Alps, drinking in the view of Switzerland, when a blast of wind threatened to blow him over the edge. His guide cried out, "Mr. Smith! On your knees, sir! The only way you're safe up here is on your knees!"[75] Similarly, when battling Satan, the only way you're safe here is on your knees.

"True," states C. H. Spurgeon, "He [God] regards not high looks and lofty words; He cares not for the pomp and pageantry of kings; He listens not to the swell of martial music; He regards not the triumph and pride of man; but wherever there is a heart big with sorrow or a lip quivering with agony or a deep groan or a penitential sigh, the heart of Jehovah is open; He marks it down in the registry of His memory; He puts our prayers, like rose leaves, between the pages of His book of remembrance; and when the volume is opened at last, there shall be a precious fragrance springing up therefrom."[76]

To put on the Armor of God, a believer needs to pray it on. It is an encouraging and fruitful exercise to do this literally each day. You might want to try using a prayer similar to the one I use:

Heavenly Father, thank You for the armor provided for my victory today. By faith, I put on the Belt of Truth that I might live what I believe and advocate. Keep me from being a castaway by helping me to maintain my integrity. By faith, I put on the Breastplate of Righteousness that I may start this day clean and holy, prepared to live a life pleasing to You. By faith, I put on the Gospel Shoes that I may be surefooted in battle against Satan, assured of my salvation and my eternal destiny and ever ready to serve. By faith, I put on the Shield of Faith, trusting You to extinguish the fiery darts of opposition that Satan hurls upon me. I will not fear what may happen today, for Thou art a shield of protection unto me. By faith, I place the Helmet of Salvation upon my head to protect my mind from carnal thoughts and to focus on the completion of my salvation in Heaven. Lord, today I look for Your coming and my departure to Heaven. By faith, I pick up the Sword of the Spirit, Thy Holy Word, to drive Satan back and to overcome temptation. By faith, I pray each piece of this protective armor upon my life that I may be a victorious Christian soldier. Grant it, O Lord, I pray, in Jesus' name. Amen.

Commenting on Joshua 7:18, C. H. Spurgeon states, "Our warfare is with evil within us and around us, and we ought to be persuaded that we are able to get the victory and that we shall do so in the name of the Lord Jesus. We are not riding for a fall, but to win; and win we shall. The grace of God in its omnipotence is put forth for the overflow of evil in every form—hence the certainty of triumph."

ASK YOURSELF

What are the seven pieces of armor a Christian is to put on daily in order to be victorious over the schemes of the Devil?

What does each piece of armor do for a believer?

Describe the two Swords mentioned in Scripture?

Which Sword are believers to use in spiritual combat? Why?

Is there armor for the back?

When and how is the armor to be put on?

What piece of armor is to be used to protect fellow soldiers of the faith, and how might it function?

Characterize the kind of prayer that God regards, according to Spurgeon.

13   Every Christian's Job

"So thou, O son of man, I have set thee a watchman unto the house of Israel; therefore thou shalt hear the word at my mouth, and warn them from me. When I say unto the wicked, O wicked man, thou shalt surely die; if thou dost not speak to warn the wicked from his way, that wicked man shall die in his iniquity; but his blood will I require at thine hand. Nevertheless, if thou warn the wicked of his way to turn from it; if he do not turn from his way, he shall die in his iniquity; but thou hast delivered thy soul."—Ezekiel 33:7–9.

Your witness can reach out and grab someone like a "grappling hook." When a "grappling hook" takes hold, it tears the flesh to pull away. The object must allow itself to be pulled in. Likewise, there is persuasive power in the Spirit-filled witness. Those who refuse might even compensate for the convicting pain you have caused them and vocally lash out at you. Others will be brought to the Lord. But no one is likely to ignore you![77]—James Mahoney

Witness by Works

"Whenever we see someone in need," writes John Stott, "whether that need is spiritual or physical or social, if we have the wherewithal to meet it, we must do so; otherwise, we cannot claim to have God's love dwelling in us (1 John 3:16). Often people have more than one need, and if we love them with God's love, we shall do our utmost to relieve their needs. It is then, too, that they are most likely to believe.

"Verbal witness is not enough. As Jesus said, it is when people 'see our good works' that our light shines most brightly and will give glory to our heavenly father (Matthew 5:16)."[78]

Envelop your verbal witness of Christ Jesus with compassion for the whole man, not just the soul. Hear Jesus: "'For I was hungry, and you fed me. I was thirsty, and you gave me a drink. I was a stranger, and you invited me into your home. I was naked, and you gave me clothing. I was sick, and you cared for me. I was in prison, and you visited me.' Then these righteous ones will reply, 'Lord, when did we ever see you hungry and feed you? Or thirsty and give you something to drink? Or a stranger and show you hospitality? Or naked and give you clothing? When did we ever see you sick or in prison and visit you?' And the King will say, 'I tell you the truth, when you did it to one of the least of these my brothers and sisters, you were doing it to me!'" (Matthew 25:35–40 NLT).

Man does not care what we have to share until he first knows how much we care. Social endeavors do not replace verbal witness; they simply undergird it and give a bridge over which to walk with the Gospel into the sinner's heart.

Witness by Words

Works must be coupled with words to win souls to the Savior. It is a solemn thought to know that "the soul and eternity of one man depends upon the voice of another."[79]

You and I are to give verbal warning to the unsaved who are traveling the broad road of meaninglessness and opposition to God about its tragic end, providing them with the opportunity of salvation. "And of some have compassion, making a difference: and others save with fear, pulling them out of the fire; hating even the garment spotted by the flesh" (Jude 22–23).

Winnie the Pooh had a donkey friend named Eeyore. Eeyore was playing too close to the water's edge, fell in and began to drown. Unable to get to the bank, he began to float downstream on his back anticipating this ride would be his last, knowing that the river ended in a waterfall.

As Eeyore floated underneath a bridge, he saw Winnie standing upon it, and a conversation ensued. Winnie said to Eeyore, "Seems like you've got yourself in a spot of trouble."

"Yes," Eeyore replied.

Winnie then said, "And it looks like you are going to drown."

Eeyore again answered sadly, "Yes." Then, with a pleading cry, Eeyore said to Winnie the Pooh, "If it wouldn't be too much bother, would you mind rescuing me?"[80]

All around us are friends, family members, and classmates who are floating downstream, not toward a waterfall, but toward eternal destruction in Hell, in need of rescue. They are not apt to rescue themselves. You and I stand on the bridge, like Winnie the Pooh, and hear their cry, "If it wouldn't be too much bother, would you mind rescuing me?"

Lee Strobel states, "Almost every day we come to evangelistic turning points. We make choices whether to help rescue these people from danger or to walk the other way. We make spur-of-the-moment decisions whether to heroically venture into their lives and lead them to a place of spiritual safety or merely hope that someone else will do it. We make split-second decisions all the time to play it safe or tilt the conversation toward spiritual topics, and many times we shrink back."[81]

A retracing of our steps today would probably shockingly reveal just how many times, in fact, we chose to shrink back from talking to an Eeyore about Christ. Who is, by their life and lips, saying to you, "If it wouldn't be too much bother, would you mind rescuing me?"

The Way to Salvation

In confronting others with the Gospel, make sure that not only is the message clear (John 3:16), but the means are correct.

There is only one way whereby man may be reconciled to God, and the means are "repentance toward God, and faith toward our Lord Jesus Christ" (Acts 20:21).

A railroad crossing employee had the responsibility of warning automobile drivers of oncoming trains by waving a lantern at the crossing. One night a train collided with a vehicle, and lives were lost. This employee was taken to court, accused of gross neglect for failure to give warning.

At the trial, the prosecutor asked the employee if he had waved a lantern at the crossing. The man answered he had. Upon acquittal, he yet was distraught. His attorney, believing he was just feeling bad for what had happened, tried to calm him by asking, "You were at the crossing in time to warn of the incoming train, correct?"

He answered, "Yes, I was."

"You waved the lantern at the crossing did you not?"

He again replied, "Yes, I did."

"Then what is troubling you?"

The man answered, "It is true that I was at the crossing and that I was waving the lantern, but my lantern was not lit."

Too many Christian students are carrying unlit lanterns to school, to social and athletic events, and to church—lanterns without the oil of the knowledge of the means and way of salvation. As with the railroad employee, it matters not how zealously you wave the gospel lantern to warn others of the consequences of rejection of Christ, if it is void of the life-changing oil necessary for man's salvation.

"Give me oil in my lamp; keep it burning, burning, burning.
Give me oil in my lamp I pray.
Give me oil in my lamp; keep it burning, burning, burning.
Keep it burning till the break of day."[82]

Praying for the Unsaved

"Our families, our schools, our congregations," writes Horatius Bonar, "not to speak of our cities at large, our land, our world, might well send us daily to our knees; for the loss of even one soul is terrible beyond conception! Eye has not seen, nor ear heard, nor has entered the heart of man, what a soul in Hell must suffer forever. Lord, give us bowels of mercies!"[83]

How might you pray for the lost (Psalm 2:8)? Pray for *Cultivation* prior to the witness, that the soil in the soul of the sinner may be broken up, seeded, and prepared for the presentation of the Gospel (Hosea 10:12).

Pray for *Orchestration* of the witness, that the Holy Spirit will lead the right believer to this person at the most opportune time to share the Gospel (Matthew 9:38).

Pray for *Reception* to the witness, that the sinner will be open to the soul winner's presentation.

Pray for *Illumination* in the witness, that the Holy Spirit will open blinded eyes that divine truth may be revealed and received (Acts 26:18; Acts 16:14).

Pray for *Liberation* in the witness, that every Satanic stronghold in the heart would be destroyed, resulting in total deliverance (Matthew 12:29).

Pray for *Conviction* in the witness, that the sinner will see his sinful disobedience toward God (John 16:8).

Pray for *Conversion* in the witness, that the lost person may express godly sorrow regarding his crime against God and in faith receive Jesus Christ as Lord and Savior (Acts 20:21). God's promise is that if we pray for the unsaved He will "give [us] the heathen for [our] inheritance" (Psalm 2:8).

A fire in a Honduras prison killed over 300 inmates. Most of the lives lost could have been saved had the guards not misplaced the keys to the prison cells.[84] Sadly, multitudes in Satan's prison will perish in everlasting fire due to the fact that most Christians either have misplaced the Gospel key or neglected its use (Acts 1:8; John 8:36) in their behalf. It's high time that Christian students find the key and use it.

ASK YOURSELF

·   What are the two means of witnessing?

How must the two link together to be effective in reaching the unsaved?

Have you been waving an unlit or extremely dim lantern? Take steps to fill your lantern with the oil of the knowledge of the means of salvation and the presentation of it to the eternally lost.

Is it a "bother" to talk to friends who are unsaved about Jesus?

According to Strobel, what are evangelistic turning points?

Describe a time when you experienced such a turning point.

What spiritual lesson may be drawn from the tragedy in the Honduras prison?

Will you today talk to the Eeyores that surround you about Jesus?

Are you regularly praying for the lost on your campus and in your neighborhood? If not, why not?

Do you believe God will keep His promise regarding praying for the lost?

14   Soul-Winning Distractions

"Say not ye, There are yet four months, and then cometh harvest? behold, I say unto you, Lift up your eyes, and look on the fields; for they are white already to harvest."—John 4:35.

Let's quit fiddling with religion and do something to bring the world to Christ.[85]—Billy Sunday

Souls were the focus of Jesus' life, and that must be the focus of the body of Christ as well. We can learn from His example and be fueled with His burning passion for the eternally lost. Jesus began His work as an Evangelist by winning Andrew and sending him out to win souls. Next, He won Phillip and dispatched him to win Nathaniel. For three years following that, in sermon, personal encounters, and Bible teaching, Jesus dealt with lost man. He witnessed to the likes of Nicodemus, Zacchaeus, Bartimaeus, and the woman at the well, as well as to the Pharisees, publicans, priests, soldiers, children—even kings. Day and night His focus was for the lost. He witnessed to all classes of people. He refused to let racial or cultural barriers impede His witness.[86] He refused to let man or schedule or opposition douse that burning flame for the lost. Scripture records nineteen personal soul-winning encounters of Jesus. He didn't just tell us to do it; He did it!

To have a focus for souls like Jesus you must do four things that He did.

You must see as Jesus saw.

What did Jesus see? Matthew 9:36 states, "But when he saw the multitudes, he was moved with compassion on them, because they fainted, and were scattered abroad, as sheep having no shepherd." What do you see when you look at classmates, athletes, teachers, family members, and waiters? Do you see just people, or do you see souls for which Jesus died who stand in desperate need of what only He can give them? Do you see them as Jesus sees them—"as sheep having no shepherd," spiritually lost and condemned to a Devil's Hell? Look at sinners through the lenses of Christ our Savior and be inflamed with a burden for them as He manifested.

You must feel as Jesus felt.

As Jesus looked upon the multitude, He was moved with compassion (verse 36). If we are going to impact our world, change our schools, and win our friends and acquaintances, we must not only see as Jesus saw, but also feel as Jesus felt for the lost.

A famous surgeon was asked, "Do you fear a day when your hands will no longer be able to operate?"

He replied, "No, I fear the day when my heart no longer feels the suffering of those I operate on." Guys, that's the day you must fear! Fear the day when your heart becomes callous and indifferent to those dying and going to Hell around you.

Heinrich Heine, the German philosopher and poet, in a time of distress stood before the statue of Venus of Milo and cried, "Ah, yes! I suppose you would help me if you could, but you can't. Your lips are still, and your heart is cold."[87]

I wonder how many hurting, lonely, troubled, doubting, and discouraged people look to Christians saying the exact same thing. Sadly, many believers are unable to help them because they lack the compassion required. All too often, believers' 'lips are still and hearts are cold' toward the lost. We need to cry, "Set my soul afire, Lord, for the lost in sin. Give to me a passion as I seek to win. Help me not to falter; never let me fail. Fill me with Thy Spirit; let Thy will prevail."[88]

You must pray as Jesus prayed.

No doubt if we see as Jesus saw and feel as He felt for the lost, we will pray as He prayed for them. He exhorts, "Pray ye therefore the Lord of the harvest, that he will send forth labourers into his harvest" (verse 38). We are to pray for the lost and also for the willingness of saints to share Jesus with them. C. H. Spurgeon said, "Before you talk to man about God, talk to God about man." Develop a prayer list for the lost and pray incessantly for their salvation. "It is doubtful if even a single soul is born again without travail of soul on the part of someone."[89]

You must do as Jesus did.

He planned to win souls. He always focused on bringing people face to face with their sin and need of God. Plan to win souls. You must make that a priority of your life. Intentionality in telling others of Christ is imperative.

The focus of the Christian must be that of bringing sinners to the Savior. Staying focused on winning souls takes predetermined commitment. It takes constant attention. You must constantly fight a natural drift away from it. I've noticed nine things against which one must always be on guard because they will cause a Christian to lose this focus on souls.

Pessimism. This is exhibiting the mindset, "It won't do any good to tell others of Jesus." Yet our Lord said that "the fields...are white already to harvest." People are hungering and thirsting for something missing in their lives. The stories of the thousands who have been won to faith in Christ prove the value of soul winning. Each of these would in unison declare, "It does some good, for I am a life that has been changed."

Busyness. Athletics, school, dating, entertainment, amusements, and work bury and suffocate the desire to witness. Souls deserve and demand unparalleled attention due to their damnable plight. In dispatching the seventy to witness, Jesus instructed, "Don't take any money with you, nor a traveler's bag, nor an extra pair of sandals. And don't stop to greet anyone on the road" (Luke 10:4 NLT). The mission was top priority, and they must not become distracted from its completion. The believer has received the same mandate. He must not "greet anyone on the road" who would interrupt the winning of souls, nor may he become entangled with the cares of this world that would deter the work. Soul winning must be kept a priority.

In England, a man was to be hung. His mother interceded on his behalf before the king, and she prevailed in getting a pardon. The page commissioned to deliver the pardon stopped to watch a clown performing and then hurried to fulfill his errand. He arrived minutes too late. While accounting to the king, he said, "I laughed with the crowd at the clown, and the time slipped away." Many Christians are laughing at the clown and enjoying life and its pleasures as time slips away, and souls die without Jesus.

Carnality. Spurgeon said, "Fish will not be fishers. We cannot be fishers of men if we remain among men in the same element with them."[90] The separated Christian is the soul-winning Christian. Worldliness, being like the world, quenches the soul winning fire.

Ralph Connors wrote of two rival university football teams in Canada. On one of these teams was a player by the name of Cameron. He was agile, strong, and quick on the field. His team was assured of victory merely by his playing in that big game. However, the night before the game, he broke training rules and got drunk. The next day, instead of being the help of his team, he was their hurt. That game went down in the annals of that school's record books as a game they had every right to win, but lost because Cameron was unfit. Concerning your opportunities to win a soul to Christ, how often is it written in God's record books that you failed because of being spiritually "unfit"?

Lack of perception regarding of Hell. The degree to which you comprehend the reality of Hell and all its torment will have much to do with the degree of focus on souls you exhibit. Eye has not seen, nor has ear heard, nor has it entered into the heart of man the torment and suffering one in Hell experiences.

R. A. Torrey well said, "A man's usefulness or uselessness depends upon what he believes about and the stand he takes on the facts of Hell. But a man who accepts that part of the Bible which he wants to accept and which he calls agreeable to his thinking, and rejects that part which he does not want to accept, in plain unvarnished language, is a fool!"[91]

Rationalization. This is thinking that somebody else will do it. We lose focus in soul winning when we pass the buck to the next guy to tell people about Jesus. I revised the anonymous poem "Somebody Else" to apply it to soul winning.

> There's a burdened young man named "Somebody Else";
> There is no one he won't witness to.
> He is busy from morning 'til way late at night,
> Talking to souls, substituting for you.
>
> You're asked to talk to Jim or to Joan,
> And what is the ready reply?
> "Get 'Somebody Else'; I'm too busy.
> He can witness to them much better than I!"
>
> There's so much to do in the harvest field,
> So much and the workers so few;
> And "Somebody Else" is weary and worn,
> Just substituting for you!

So next opportunity to share the faith,
Come back with this ready reply:
"'Somebody Else' can't reach the dying lost alone.
I gladly will work by his side."

Don't depend upon "Somebody Else" witnessing to the neighbor, work associate, teammate, classmate, or family member; do it yourself.

Inactivity. When we fail to tell of Christ, it clouds the need to focus on the pursuit of souls. Going and telling fuels our focus on the soul winning task.

Unbiblical premise. To believe God has already pre-determined who will go to Heaven and who will go to Hell certainly extinguishes one's focus on evangelism. "I do not see," Adrian Rogers stated, "where it [the Bible] teaches that God preselects some to salvation and consigns the rest of humanity to eternal damnation without ever making them a sincere offer of forgiveness."[92] All may be saved who are willing to be saved. If you don't tell, men will go to Hell.

Indifference. William Barclay states, "The problem of modern evangelism is not hostility to Christianity; it would be better if it were so." The problem, according to Barclay, is that Christians regard the lost with complete indifference.[93]

Evangelistic indifference is the great sin of the church and one of the most difficult to combat. A great pastor revealed that in times of evangelistic indifference, he went soul winning to rekindle the spark. "I believe," states F. B. Myer, "that if there is one thing which pierces the Master's heart with unutterable grief, it is not the world's iniquity, but the Church's indifferences."[94]

Absence of its being pushed in the church. The failure of ministers and leaders to keep soul winning prominent among

Christians lessens the focus. D. L. Moody, in an effort to keep soul winning prominent before the members of his church, hung on the exit doors a sign that read, "You are now entering the mission field of the world. Go soul winning." Preachers should share personal soul-winning stories in their sermons and preach on soul winning; singers should sing songs about soul winning; teachers should teach about soul winning; soul winning workshops should be offered with outreach nights scheduled.

Determine not to lose your focus on souls. I don't know of a more exacting song that depicts the Christian duty regarding the lost than *O Zion, Haste* written by Mary A. Thompson during the grave illness of her son. This hymn pulsates with the urgent and compelling need to tell the unreached people of the world "of the Savior's dying or of the life He died for them to win." Why? "That He who made all nations is not willing one soul should perish, lost in shades of night." Ponder that statement: "Not willing one soul should perish." Sound familiar? Peter uttered the same (2 Peter 3:9). God is not willing *anyone* perish—not your boyfriend or girlfriend, not your parent, not your sibling, not your friend, not your teacher, not the elite, not the poor, not the Hitlers or the Mansons, not anyone—so stay soul focused!

A child was lost in a vast wheat field. Friends and rescue helpers searched diligently until the dark forced them to halt for the night. The next morning as they resumed their search, the suggestion was made that they join hands and form an unbroken human chain across the field in search for the child. In doing this, they found the lost child, but tragically it was too late. The child's mother walked back and forth wringing her hands and crying, "Why didn't we join hands sooner? Why didn't we join hands sooner?" The lost are all about us. It is high time believers in united focus join hands in rescuing them before it is eternally too late. Will you join hands with fellow believers in this soul-saving rescue attempt?

ASK YOURSELF

What is your focus of life?

What was the focus of Jesus' life?

Name the four things that He did that you must do to exhibit that same focus on souls.

Of the nine reasons stated by which a person loses focus on souls, which five do you identify with the most, and why?

What steps may be taken to avoid these five things?

Why is it important to tell others the gospel message?

What can the church do to encourage soul focus?

15   Spiritual Coaching

"And let us consider and give attentive, continuous care to watching over one another, studying how we may stir up (stimulate and incite) to love and helpful deeds and noble activities."– Hebrews 10:24, Amplified

"So, being affectionately desirous of you, we were ready to share with you not only the gospel of God but also our own selves, because you had become very dear to us."—The Apostle Paul (1 Thessalonians 2:8 ESV)

When you mentor leaders who mentor others, you extend your influence as a mentoring leader on to generations you may never see.[95]—The Good Book on Leadership

The growth and development of people is the highest calling of leadership.[96]—Harvey S. Firestone

Barnabas took Paul under his wing while Paul was just a babe in Christ and developed him in the things of Christ. "But Barnabas took him [Paul], and brought him to the apostles, and declared unto them how he had seen the Lord in the way, and that he had spoken to him, and how he had preached boldly at Damascus in the name of Jesus" (Acts 9:27). The words "took him" literally mean that Barnabas physically held on to Paul to help him. The Apostle Paul would not have become what he was for God had it not been for Barnabas' mentorship in his early life.

Solomon said, "Iron sharpeneth iron" (Proverbs 27:17). The Lord counts on spiritually mature believers to sharpen young Christians in doctrine, devotion, and duty until they then can do the same for someone else. Young Christians—and anyone going into ministry—should seek out a godly person to be a spiritual coach.

(Note: Mentors and disciples should always be of the same sex.) The spiritually mature must now, more than ever, invest in new and immature believers, allowing rivers of spiritual knowledge and experience to flow into and through them.

An excellent pattern for mentoring (spiritually coaching) is found in the relationship of the Apostle Paul to Timothy (2 Timothy 1–3). Paul models seven key components of effective mentoring.

(1) Conviction (1:11). The blind cannot lead the blind. It is imperative that the mentor be a person of biblical soundness, separation, and surrender. John MacArthur, in *The Footsteps of Faith,* comments on the power of example. "Thomas Brooks said, 'Example is the most powerful rhetoric.' He was right. The single greatest tool of spiritual leadership is the power of an exemplary life. Along with the principles for living that the Bible gives us, we need models to follow because we tend to be creatures led more by pattern than precept. We are better at following a pattern or a model than we are at fleshing out a precept or principle. What makes examples so powerful? Why is it 'the most powerful rhetoric'? An example shows us what principles can't."[97]

(2) Confirmation (1:5–6). The infusion of confidence and certainty regarding salvation and the ministry call by the mentor is essential. The coach has to help the disciple believe in him- or herself.

(3) Cultivation (1:13; 3:14). This requires imparting God's Word to the soul and watering it until it sprouts. The mentor must constantly sow sound biblical doctrine and teaching into the disciple. The spiritual coach must be as a "barking dog" to the disciple, continuously warning of potential "snares," heresy, and soul neglect.

(4) Correction (1:7). The mentor must confront moral and spiritual faults and weaknesses (Galatians 6:1). Mentors hold their disciples accountable—morally, ethically, and spiritually.

96

(5) Commendation (1:3). The display of approval in lessons learned and battles won encourages the disciple to press forward. Imagine how Timothy's heart must have raced in hearing that a spiritual giant like Paul thanked God for him and believed in him. Give praise when praise is due.

(6) Clarification (2:16–19). The mentor's task is to clear up any misunderstanding or misinterpretation regarding Scripture or personal decisions made.

(7) Compulsion (1:14; 2:3; 2:22; 3:14; 4:1–5). The spiritual coach must compel, incite, and motivate the disciple to keep a tight grip on "that good thing [the Gospel] which was committed unto [him] by the Holy Ghost" (1:14). The disciple must be taught patience and persistence and must see his or her potential, despite suffering, persecution, failure, or discouragement. Mentors must exhort disciples never to quit or to give up on the faith or the divine call.

ASK YOURSELF

If the apostle Paul needed a spiritual mentor (Barnabas) and Timothy needed a mentor (Paul), don't you?

Who might qualify to be invited to be such a coach?

Based upon Paul's example in mentoring Timothy, summarize the role of the mentor.

If you are spiritually mature, grounded in the faith, who might you help grow spiritually by being their coach?

What does the phrase "iron sharpeneth iron" mean?

16   Three Kinds of People

"Brothers and sisters, in the past I could not talk to you as I talk to spiritual people. I had to talk to you as I would to people without the Spirit—babies in Christ. The teaching I gave you was like milk, not solid food, because you were not able to take solid food. And even now you are not ready. You are still not spiritual, because there is jealousy and quarreling among you, and this shows that you are not spiritual. You are acting like people of the world."—1 Corinthians 3:1–3 NLT

The whole life of a Christian should be nothing but praises and thanks to God; we should neither eat nor sleep, but eat to God and sleep to God and work to God and talk to God, do all to His glory and praise.[98]—Richard Sibbes

Lukewarmness is not weakness; it is wickedness. It is not a small sin; it's a great sin. If the greatest commandment is to love God with all your heart, then the greatest sin is not to do so. In the last days, our Lord says that lukewarmness will be the condition of the average church.[99]—Adrian Rogers

The Bible categorizes people into three groups—natural, spiritual, and carnal. The category in which you fit reveals your present spiritual relationship and walk with Christ.

Are You a Natural Man?

The natural man is described by Jesus as one who is spiritually dead. This is a good analogy, for the spiritually dead (unsaved) bear similar traits to the physically dead in three ways. The dead have no appetite, no activity, and no awareness. First, the natural man has no appetite for spiritual things, because that which creates it is absent from his life. Second, the natural man has no activity spiritually. He may attend church, but solid commitment to Christ is missing. Third, the natural man has no awareness of his condition. He is spiritually blind to his present and future plight, and to either the reality of Christ or his need of Christ.

Nicodemus is a picture of the natural man. John 3 shares about his encounter with Jesus. Nicodemus, in confronting Jesus, asked, "'How can a man be born when he is old? Can he enter a second time into his mother's womb and be born?' Jesus answered, 'Truly, truly, I say to you, unless one is born of water and the Spirit, he cannot enter the kingdom of God. That which is born of the flesh is flesh, and that which is born of the Spirit is spirit. Do not marvel that I said to you, "You must be born again." The wind blows where it wishes, and you hear its sound, but you do not know where it comes from or where it goes. So it is with everyone who is born of the Spirit'" (John 3:4–8 ESV). Nicodemus just couldn't understand the meaning of the new birth, despite the simplicity of Jesus' presentation.

C. H. Spurgeon understood well why Nicodemus didn't grasp what Jesus was saying. Declared Spurgeon: "The unregenerate heart can no more understand the Gospel than a horse can understand astronomy. It is altogether beyond the comprehension of the carnal man....Spiritual things must be spiritually discerned."[100]

In order for a man to be made alive to the physical world, there must be a physical birth. Likewise, for a man to be made alive to the spiritual realm, there must be a spiritual birth. Not until the natural man is "born again" will he possess an appetite, activity, and awareness spiritually.

Two sisters were at a storefront window seeking to describe a beautiful dress to their blind sister. In describing its color and design, they asked her, "Don't you see it?"

To this she replied, "No, I cannot." The best description a Christian can give to the unsaved of the grandeur of the Christian life is beyond their comprehension, because they "just can't see it." The Christian must rely upon the Holy Spirit to open the blinded eyes of the natural man that he may see and believe. Are you a natural man?

Are You a Spiritual Man?

The spiritual man has been born twice—physically and spiritually. It has been said that he who is born once dies twice, and he who is born twice dies once. This type of man was a natural man but was made alive in Jesus Christ through the new birth.

There are six distinguishing marks of the spiritual man.

Devotion. He manifests an intimate love relationship with Christ.

Discipline. He beats his body into subjection to the things of God, refusing to do what comes naturally.

Duty. He is actively engaged in Christian work and bears fruit.

Discernment. He sees through spiritual lenses and is able to make moral and spiritual decisions based upon God's Word. He sees things from God's perspective.

Domination. He lives under the control and dominion of the Holy Spirit. The mind of Christ is manifest in him more and more. He is a Spirit-filled and directed believer.

Difference. He lives differently from the world and those in the church who live subpar Christian lives. Some count him weird because of the stance he takes on separation from the world. Are you a spiritual man?

Are You a Carnal Man?

If you are not a natural or spiritual man, then you fit the final category of carnality. The carnal man is a Christian, but an immature Christian. He is yet a baby spiritually when he should have matured into adulthood.

Like a baby, the carnal believer is shallow in knowledge. Babies have limited understanding and knowledge. Are you shallow or deep in Bible knowledge and understanding?

Like a baby, the carnal believer is easily offended. Babies are very sensitive and get their feelings hurt easily. Does this describe you when things don't go your way at home or with friends?

Like a baby, the carnal believer has trouble staying clean. Ask any parent if this is not true. Wash, clean, and dress up a baby, and, if left to himself, in no time he will be dirty again. Are you like this? Are you walking in cleanliness before God, or do you find yourself having to take a lot of baths? Are you getting dirty with pornography, acts of impurity, dishonesty, drugs, or alcohol?

Like a baby, the carnal believer throws food off the table. I saw a baby throw food he didn't want back at his father at an IHOP restaurant. Does this picture you? When the student minister or pastor puts on your plate sound teaching that goes against your lifestyle, do you throw it back and refuse to eat it?

In summary, the carnal man is a dwarfed Christian. He fails to grow, develop, or mature spiritually. The carnal man is a defeated Christian unable to conquer sin continuously, for he lacks spiritual power. The carnal man is a disobedient Christian allowing impure thoughts and activities to occur. The carnal man is a dependent Christian relying upon preachers and teachers to spoonfeed him the Word of God and keep him straight. He lives on a spiritual roller coaster with highs and lows, ups and downs, in walking with Jesus on a continual basis.

The Laodicean church consisted of carnal people. To these Jesus said, "So then because thou art lukewarm, and neither cold nor hot, I will spue [vomit] thee out of my mouth" (Revelation 3:16). There is a cost for remaining carnal. Are you a carnal man?

Which of these three kinds of people are you?

ASK YOURSELF

In what three ways is the natural man like a corpse?

What is necessary for the natural man to "see" and to "live" spiritually?

In what ways is the carnal man like a baby? Why?

What are the distinguishing traits of the spiritual man?

How might a person become a spiritual man?

17   Understanding God's Will

"And the LORD shall guide thee continually."—Isaiah 58:11.

The decisions you make, small and great, do to your life what the sculptor's chisel does to his block of marble. You are shaping your life by your thoughts, attitudes, and actions.[101]—Warren Wiersbe

Like Enoch, walk with God, and you cannot mistake your road. You have infallible wisdom to direct you, immutable love to comfort you, and eternal power to defend you. "Jehovah"—mark the word—"Jehovah shall guide thee continually."[102]—C. H. Spurgeon

The will of God—nothing less, nothing more, nothing else.[103]—F. E. Marsh

"Created in Christ Jesus unto good works, which God hath before ordained that we should walk in them" (Ephesians 2:10). "Created in Christ Jesus" means the Christian has a new life through the new birth in Christ Jesus. "Unto good works" means every believer is saved to engage in a life of service. "Which God hath before ordained" means God designed this life of service in ages past. "That we should walk in them" means this plan of service is knowable and doable. All through this great text runs the pivotal theme that God has a plan for every life in Christ Jesus.

In the New Testament, the Greek word for "call" occurs about 150 times, referencing for most part God's call to man.[104] Every Christian is "called" to serve God in a general sense, while some are "called" to serve Him in a specific sense as vocational servants. Paul states in Ephesians 4:11–12, "And he gave some, apostles; and some, prophets; and some, evangelists; and some, pastors and teachers; For the perfecting of the saints, for the work of the ministry, for the edifying of the body of Christ."

How can a believer know if God is extending a call into full-time Christian service? It is easy to be puzzled over this thing we designate as a "call." How does it come? How do you know when it comes? When does it come? How do you say yes to it when it comes? God's will is neither vague nor hidden but readily knowable.

Discovery of God's will for your life is pivotal to living in the arena of maximum usefulness, happiness, and peace. "See then that ye walk circumspectly, not as fools, but as wise, Redeeming the time, because the days are evil. Wherefore be ye not unwise, but understanding what the will of the Lord is" (Ephesians 5:15–17).

Alice in Wonderland, upon inquiring about directions of the Cheshire cat, was asked, "Where do you want to go?"

She replied, "It doesn't matter."

The cat responded, "Then it doesn't matter which way you go."[105] Direction in life matters to the Christian, or at least it ought to. It matters enormously which way you go.

A man walking behind a gipsy woman noticed that when they came to a place where the road divided, she threw her stick up into the air and let it fall on the ground. This she did a second time and a third time. Soon the traveling man caught up with her and, being curious, inquired, "Why do you throw your stick up into the air like that?"

She replied, "That is how I determine which way to go; I go whichever way the stick points."

"But you threw it up three times," he said, wondering why she had done so.

"Yes, I did," she answered, "for the silly thing would point that way, and I wanted it to go this way!"

106

The lesson is obvious. To truly know the will of God, you must stop tossing the stick in the air and yield absolutely to whatever direction He leads without question. This is the essential step in ascertaining the will of God.

Knowing which way to go requires time spent in God's presence with a clean heart, listening ears, a submissive spirit, and ready feet. It is not to the "casual" Christian that God's will is manifest, but to the committed Christian (Romans 12:1–2).

Keep stoking the fire for God in your soul so that when He speaks, you will hear. The more you work at knowing God intimately and loving Him passionately, the easier it will be to recognize His voice. Max Lucado expands on this truth.

"We learn God's will by spending time in His presence. The key to knowing God's heart is having a relationship with Him—a personal relationship. God will speak to you differently than He will speak to others. Just because God spoke to Moses through a burning bush, that doesn't mean we should all sit next to a bush waiting for God to speak. God used a fish to convict Jonah. Does that mean we should have worship services at Sea World? No. God reveals His heart personally to each person. For that reason, your walk with God is essential. His heart is not seen in an occasional chat or weekly visit. We learn His will as we take up residence in His house every single day. Walk with him long enough, and you come to know His heart."[106]

In *Reckless Faith,* John MacArthur emphasizes that when a believer walks in the revealed will of God, which encompasses that we be saved (1 Timothy 2:3–4), we be Spirit-filled (Ephesians 5:17–18), we be sanctified (1 Thessalonians 4:3), we be submissive (1 Peter 2:13–15), and we suffer (1 Peter 4:19; Philippians 1:29; 2 Timothy 3:12),[107] he will have little difficulty ascertaining God's specific will about other matters.

Spiritual Markers

Spiritual markers are helpful in understanding God's will. Genesis 13:3–4 says of Abraham:

"And he went on his journeys from the south even to Bethel, unto the place where his tent had been at the beginning, between Bethel and Hai; Unto the place of the altar, which he had made there at the first: and there Abram called on the name of the LORD."

After living in Egypt, Abraham returned to the place where he had previously called upon the name of the Lord. This was a spiritual marker in his life.

Spiritual markers can be places or reference points which identify a transition, decision, or direction when God clearly gave guidance.[108] In looking at these markers, a person can readily see the direction God is moving his or her life. These markers are important in understanding God's guidance. When you encounter a new marker along the way (a call to ministry, for example), it is helpful to look at the previous markers you've encountered. If they all seem to point in the same direction, then you are most likely moving in the right direction.

The Holy Spirit

A major role of the Holy Spirit is to guide us (John 16:13) in the knowledge of God's will. He is omniscient, omnipresent, and infallible; therefore, most qualified. He never has disappointed nor led astray the believer who has sought His counsel; therefore, He is to be trusted. Spurgeon states, "The Holy Spirit teaches us in three ways: suggestion, direction, and illumination. There are thoughts that dwell in our minds that are suggestions put there by the Spirit for us to follow. Sometimes He leads us by direction, leading our thoughts along into a more excellent channel than that which we started. Sometimes He leads us by illuminating the Word of God to us."[109]

Wait for the Green Light

If you are patient by waiting before God in prayer for His divine communication, clarification, and confirmation, He will reveal what you seek. David sought God's will regarding an upcoming battle. At the sound of the rumbling of the mulberry trees, David was told to attack the enemy, and not until (1 Chronicles 14:13–15). Let us learn from David to take no steps without God. Wait until the rumbling of the mulberry trees is heard (i.e., God's sign, confirmation), and then proceed, but not prior to that.

To help focus your heart, try personalizing this straightforward prayer:

"Shew me thy ways, O LORD; teach me thy paths. Lead me in thy truth, and teach me: for thou art the God of my salvation; on thee do I wait all the day" (Psalm 25:4–5).

How can one know if God has specifically set him or her apart for vocational Christian service?

The Appeal of the Soul (1 Timothy 3:1)

C. H. Spurgeon identifies the first sign of the heavenly calling as "an intense, all-absorbing desire for the work. In order to [have] a true call to the ministry, there must be an irresistible, overwhelming craving and raging thirst for telling to others what God has done to our own souls."[110] With Paul, the person God calls cries, "For necessity is laid upon me; yea, woe is unto me, if I preach not the gospel!" (1 Corinthians 9:16). In the call, God puts a 'fire in the bones' to do the task He assigns that neither time, trouble, nor tribunal can quench (Jeremiah 20:9).

The Affirmation of Saints (Proverbs 11:14)

God uses His people to endorse those whom He calls to this work. When I was a sophomore in college, classmates were used of God to reveal and confirm my call into evangelism. "Yet this appeal," says Spurgeon, "is not final nor infallible and is only to be

109

estimated in proportion to the intelligence and piety of those consulted."[111]

Consult with those who are deeply spiritual, possess great discernment, and will be candid in their advisement. "Considerable weight," says Spurgeon, "is to be given to the judgment of men and women who live near to God, and in most instances their verdict will not be a mistaken one."[112]

George W. Truett, the gifted and powerful preacher of the nineteenth and twentieth centuries perhaps never would have entered the ministry had not the church raised up in unison to ordain him. Truett protested, but the congregation's pleadings forced him to relent and to submit. Speaking about that night, Truett said, "There I was against a whole church, against a church profoundly moved. There was not a dry eye in the house....one of the supremely solemn hours in a church's life. I was thrown into the stream and just had to swim." That night was the turning point in this twenty-three-year-old man's life, for he laid down the pursuit to be a lawyer and took up that to be God's minister.[113]

One but trembles to imagine what might have been had not Truett listened to God's voice through the saints that Saturday night in Whiteright, Texas. Most certainly God will extend His call to ministry *station to station* (through others) when efforts fail to do so *person to person*.

The Aptitude of Self

An honest evaluation of one's personal aptitude to minister effectively is another possible indicator of a call. In the call to evangelism, pastorate, or mission field, God gifts the person with the ability for the task. These gifts, though they may be developed to be more effective, cannot be self-acquired. With regard to a call to preach, C. H. Spurgeon stated, "Still, a man must not consider that he is called to preach until he has proved that he *can* speak....If a man be called to preach, he will be endowed with a degree of speaking ability, which he will cultivate and increase."[114]

The possession or absence of the spiritual gifts necessary for the ministry task under consideration can help discern God's will. "It seems true to say," writes John Stott, "that God seldom calls people to a wider ministry before they have first proved themselves in a narrower; and the best and most natural context in which to put to the test an incipient sense of vocation is the regular evangelistic outreach of the local church."[115]

The Agreement of Scripture

What will light the way for you regarding God's call? Psalm 19:8 answers frankly, "The statutes of the LORD are right, rejoicing the heart: the commandment of the LORD is pure, enlightening the eyes." Holy Scripture transmits light (divine knowledge) to the soul. Don't live in the dark or make decisions in the dark. Turn on the light of God's Word for illumination. "Thy word is a lamp unto my feet, and a light unto my path" (Psalm 119:105). God will never call you to do a work His Word denounces.

The Authorization of the Spirit

Taking all that has been stated into serious consideration, ultimately, in the final analysis, what constitutes a call is the seal of the Spirit, His stamp of approval. Paul declares that "the Spirit itself beareth witness with our spirit, that we are the children of God" (Romans 8:16). It is this same Spirit that will bear witness in equal measure with one's spirit that he is divinely set apart for a specific assignment. It is He that will speak the word of confirmation or not to the open and waiting heart. Spurgeon, referring to the ascending Christ's gifts to the church of pastor, evangelist, and teacher, frankly declared, "He alone can give them; any that come without Him are imposters."[116]

This much is certain—God calls all His children to be servants, whether vocationally as ministers or as laymen. All, regardless of the sphere of life's work, are called to continuously and faith-fully serve God and man. One's greater effectiveness in this service will only be known in God's divine, sanctioned, ordained sphere.

It is for our best that full knowledge of God's will regarding some things is withheld at the outset so we might walk by faith and not by sight. This also gives God time to prepare us for its disclosure, lest in its revelation, we become disheartened or doubtful.

I know not what awaits me.
God kindly veils my eyes,
And o'er each step of my onward way,
He makes new scenes to rise;
And every joy He sends me comes
A sweet and glad surprise.

Where He may lead I'll follow,
My trust in Him repose;
And every hour in perfect peace,
I'll sing, "He knows, He knows";
And every hour in perfect peace,
I'll sing, "He knows, He knows."

One step I see before me,
'Tis all I need to see;
The light of Heaven more brightly shines
When earth's illusions flee,
And sweetly through the silence comes,
His loving, "Trust in Me!"

Oh, blissful lack of wisdom—
       'Tis blessed not to know!
He holds me with His own right hand
       And will not let me go
And lulls my troubled soul to rest
       In Him who loves me so.

So on I go not knowing;
       I would not if I might.
I'd rather walk in the dark with God
       Than go alone in the light;
I'd rather walk by faith with Him
       Than go alone by sight.[117]

He knows; He knows; He knows.

ASK YOURSELF

How does Jeremiah 29:11 relate to God's will?

What essentials to knowing God's will are revealed in Romans 12:1–2?

Do you feel direction in life's matters? Why, or why not?

Have you seriously sought God's will about your life's work; and, if so, what direction do you sense Him guiding?

How might a person understand the will of God for his or her life?

List the spiritual markers of your life in sequence. What seems to be the pivotal direction in life to which they point?

Do these markers seem to confirm God's call to ministry; and, if so, will you obey?

Explain the difference between the extension of a call to ministry by God *person to person* and *station to station*?

18   The Fear Factor

"What time I am afraid, I will trust in thee. In God I will praise his word, in God I have put my trust; I will not fear what flesh can do unto me."—Psalm 56:3–4.

The man who measures things by the circumstances of the hour is filled with fear; the man who sees Jehovah enthroned and governing has no panic.[118]—G. Campbell Morgan

Fear is born of Satan, and if we would only take time to think a moment, we would see that everything Satan says is founded upon a falsehood. He is the father of lies. Even his fears are falsehoods, and his terrors ought to serve as encouragements. When Satan tells you, therefore, that some ill is going to come, you may quietly look in his face and tell him he is a liar. Instead of ill, goodness and mercy shall follow you all the days of your life. And then turn to your blessed Lord and say, "What time I am afraid, I will trust in thee" (Psalm 56:3). Every fear is distrust, and trust is the remedy for fear.[119]—A. B. Simpson

Nor is the Lord before us only; He is with us. Above, beneath, around, within is the omnipotent, omnipresent One. In all time, even to eternity, He will be with us even as He has been. How this should nerve our arm! Dash at it boldly, ye soldiers of the cross, for the Lord of hosts is with us!

Being before us and with us, He will never withdraw His help. He cannot fail in Himself, and He will not fail toward us. He will continue to help us according to our need, even to the end. As He cannot fail us, so He will not forsake us. He will always be both able and willing to grant us strength and succor till fighting days are gone. Let us not fear nor be dismayed; for the Lord of hosts will go down to the battle with us, will bear the brunt of the fight and give us the victory.[120]—C. H. Spurgeon

David was no coward, but rather one of the boldest men of history. Recall how he faced Goliath. The trained soldiers of King Saul trembled in fear before this giant, yet David fearlessly fought him in the name of the Lord with only a slingshot in his hand. On another occasion, David, with the help of three men, slew an entire Philistine army. Indeed, he was a "man's man." Yet this great warrior, this hero of Israel, this mighty man of God states that he had his times in life when he was afraid.

And who of us cannot state the same? All can testify that there are those times in life when we are struck with fear and tremble and are afraid. The fear causes anxiety, emotional chaos, sickness, and loss of realistic perspective. In such times, what are we to do? The same as David did—say, "What time I am afraid, I will trust in Thee...[and] praise his word."

What are some "what time I am afraid" situations in life?"

The "what time I am afraid" of Discovery. This is a fear that something done in the "dark" will be brought into the "light." It is fear that a past sin that was hidden will be revealed. The conscience doesn't rage with fear of such discovery all the time, but in those 'what times' it does, dread, guilt, and remorse fill the heart. At such times, say with David, "What time I am afraid of my past finding me out, I will trust in God. He promised in His Word to forgive if I asked with repentant heart, and upon these promises I stand. I will not fear what my past can do unto me."

Tremble over your sins; ever realize you deserve the deepest Hell because of them, but rest in the mercy and grace of Christ that has forgiven them. So when Satan the accuser comes whispering in your ear about stuff done ten, five, or two years ago, trust in God, plead His Word, and faint not. The sin you should fear

116

is that which has not been acknowledged to God nor forsaken. "People who conceal their sins will not prosper, but if they confess and turn from them, they will receive mercy" (Proverbs 28:13 NLT).

The "what time I am afraid" of Deception. A cloud of doubt and uncertainty hangs over many students regarding being saved, generating fear that in the end they will miss Heaven. A person who has been "born again" into the family of God can never be "unborn" (John 5:24). Jesus' promise of abundant and eternal life to all who repent and believe is certain and trustworthy (John 10:10; Acts 20:21). Satan may attack and assault the believer's faith, but he can never steal it. He can never undo what God has done in salvation. At the moment of salvation, the believer's name is written with permanent ink in the Lamb's Book of Life, and neither Satan, demons, nor man can erase it (Romans 8:31–39). Have you turned from sin to faith in Jesus Christ? Have you invited Christ Jesus into your life as Lord and Savior? If so, in times of doubting or fear, trust God and rely upon His promises.

The "what time I am afraid" of Death. The perspective of the apostle Paul on death for the Christian ought to extinguish our fear of it: "To be absent from the body, and to be present with the Lord" (2 Corinthians 5:8). Death to the Christian is but to enter into the arms of Christ Jesus!

I read a story about a boy whose work required walking home late at night through a cemetery. This was feared each night until he realized that just beyond the cemetery and the graves was home where his father was watching and waiting. There is no need to fear the cemetery or the casket, for just beyond them is Home where the Father is watching and waiting. He will make certain of your safe passage.

Why death? The prophet Isaiah stated, "The good men perish; the godly die before their time and no one seems to care or wonder why. No one seems to realize that God is taking them away from the evil days ahead. For the godly who die shall rest in peace"

(Isaiah 57:1–2 TLB). What a thought! Death is God's grace at work protecting saints who die from future heartache. Friends and relatives who die in the Lord are a trillion times better off than you and I are, for they are at peace in the presence of God.

A boy who was highly allergic to bee stings was riding in the car with his father and became terrified when a bee flew in the window. The father stopped the car, allowing the boy to get out while he caught the bee. Back in the car, the boy both saw the bee and heard it buzzing and cried out with fear once again. The boy's fear was calmed when the father simply opened his hand, revealing the bee's stinger.

Death makes a lot of fuss and noise but is powerless to harm us, for Jesus Christ bore its stinger upon the Cross. With Paul, the saint can say confidently, "O death, where is thy sting? O grave, where is thy victory? But thanks be to God, which giveth us the victory through our Lord Jesus Christ" (1 Corinthians 15:55; 57).

"In a moment, in the twinkling of an eye, at the last trump: for the trumpet shall sound, and the dead shall be raised incorruptible, and we shall be changed. For this corruptible must put on incorruption, and this mortal must put on immortality.... then shall be brought to pass the saying that is written, Death is swallowed up in victory" (1 Corinthians 15:52–54).

So in the 'what times you are afraid' of death, do as David did and say, "At what times I am afraid of death, I will trust in God, who will insure safe passage into His presence for both me and my saved loved ones."

The "what time I am afraid" of Duty. Students often limit God from what He wants to do in their lives because they are afraid of disappointment and failure. Moses feared failure in a divine assignment; all do occasionally. At times you will have to do God's work in fear, but never allow fear to keep you from doing God's work!

118

Martin Luther said that often when he went to preach, his knees knocked together for fear; but when he was preaching, he had such hope in God's mercy that he was like a lion. He obeyed despite the fear, for he hoped in God. There will be times when God assigns a task that may cause you to "shake in your boots" with fear; in such times, declare, "At what times I am afraid of failure in fulfilling God's plan or task, I will trust Him with the outcome, holding nothing back." There is never a demand upon your spirit that is not also a demand upon His Spirit within you! If God is calling you into vocational ministry, shrink not back out of fear, but trust Him to perform His good work in and through you regardless of how gigantic the challenge appears.

Sooner or later you will face these "what times I am afraid" in life. In such times, remember six things.

Remember that trust is not a feeling that all will work out for the best, but an abiding conviction based upon God's Word.

Remember to trust God, despite what circumstances seem to say. David said, "In God I will praise his word, in God I have put my trust" (Psalm 56:4). What we put in God's control is ever under His control! You can bank on that. Never allow what appears to be to generate fear that God has abandoned you or has let you down.

Remember that there is no fear from which God is incapable or unwilling to grant deliverance.

Remember that fear is induced often by a lie parading as truth. We are so afraid of crossing bridges that do not exist.

Remember that God can do anything but fail you. He says to you, "When thou liest down, thou shalt not be afraid: yea, thou shalt lie down, and thy sleep shall be sweet. Be not afraid of sudden fear, neither of the desolation of the wicked, when it cometh. For the LORD shall be thy confidence, and shall keep thy foot from being taken" (Proverbs 3:24–26).

119

Remember that everyone faces fear of some sort occasionally. Don't hesitate to talk with a student minister, pastor, or Christian counselor for support and guidance regarding fear, especially if it is persistent.

C. H. Spurgeon sums up the Christian's position in the face of adversity or persecution in commenting on Psalm 16:8: "This is the way to be safe. The Lord being ever in our minds, we come to feel safety and certainty because of His being so near. He is at our right hand to guide and aid us; and hence we are not moved by fear, nor force, nor fraud, nor fickleness. When God stands at a man's right hand, that man is himself sure to stand."[121]

ASK YOURSELF

Which of the fears referenced above resonate the most with you, and why?

Are you possessed by a fear presently; and, if so, what is it?

Who is the generator of unhealthy and devastating fears?

What are some ill effects of fear?

How is a believer to deal with fear effectively?

Look up Proverbs 3:24–26 and explain its instruction regarding fear.

19   What Kind of Christian Are You?

"I know thy works, and where thou dwellest."—Revelation 2:13.

The idea of being on fire for Christ will strike some people as dangerous emotionalism. "Surely," they say, "we are not meant to go to extremes. You are not asking us to become hot-gospel fanatics?" Well, of course, it depends what you mean. If by "fanaticism" you really mean "wholeheartedness," then Christianity is a fanatical religion, and every Christian should be a fanatic. But wholeheartedness is not the same as fanaticism. Fanaticism is an unreasoning and unintelligent wholeheartedness. It is the running away of the heart with the head.[122]—John Stott

In the book of Revelation (2:1–3:22), seven kinds of church members are revealed. Five of these are at best carnal and told to repent. The other two are commended for their devotion and love for Christ. What kind of church member are you—the kind that God commends or condemns?

<u>The Ephesus kind (2:1–7).</u> Ephesus Christians are those who have abandoned their first love for Christ and allowed their enthusiasm to wane in their walk with Christ. Should a Christian be as happy and devoted to Christ today as he was the day he was saved? Should a Christian feel as close to Christ now as he did when he was saved? Should he still have a zest in his step and a song in the heart as he did on the day he met Christ? The answer to each of these questions is most assuredly, and even more so.

However, the testimony of most students is to the contrary. Their experience of salvation is but a blurred memory in the distant past, and they no longer love Christ with the same fervency as at the start. Exactly what Jesus forewarned the disciples about has happened in our generation. He said, "And because iniquity shall abound, the love of many shall wax cold" (Matthew 24:12). He does not say that "zeal shall wax cold," though it surely has; or that "doctrine shall grow unorthodox" (more liberal), though indeed it has; but that a love for Christ, His church, His people, His Book, His cause would wax cold. Has your love for the person of Christ waxed cold, cooled down from the burning inferno of past days? If so, then you are called on to repent and return to your first love.

Guard your *love for* Christ, not just the *things of* Christ. The Ephesus Christians are both a solemn reminder and a sober warning to us, lest we, as they, allow our love for Christ to "slip." Christ wants a believer's heart as well as his hands and head.

The Smyrna kind (2:8–11). A Smyrna Christian is the kind who for Christ's sake suffers persecution due to convictions and commitments. Saints of the Smyrna church were imprisoned, lost personal property, and some even died in their stand for Christ. John reveals that though these saints were extremely poor materialistically, they were extremely rich in Christ. Are you a Smyrna Christian, standing for Christ despite the persecution it brings?

Jesus said, "Blessed are ye, when men shall revile you, and persecute you, and shall say all manner of evil against you falsely, for my sake" (Matthew 5:11). Amidst the persecution, remember that you are standing shoulder to shoulder with Christ and all His children who are tormented for standing firm. Count it a joy when suffering is required for His name's sake. Are you a Smyrna Christian, or do you cower down and retreat in the face of opposition? When did you last take a stand that cost something dearly prized? Christ needs more students with spiritual backbone to stand tall for biblical values regardless of cost or consequence.

The Pergamos kind (2:12–17). Pergamos Christians are those who allow liberals from outside the church to adulterate

124

biblical beliefs and values within the church. Such liberals advocate that almost anything is acceptable regarding belief and conduct. Are you listening to liberals or unbelievers and buying into what they teach? If so, you are a Pergamos Christian to whom Christ says, "Repent; or else I will come unto thee quickly, and will fight against them with the sword of my mouth" (Revelation 2:16). God will not tolerate compromise with the world among His people.

The Thyatira kind (2:18–29). Jezebel was a self-acclaimed prophetess who taught believers to engage in acts of sexual immorality and to eat food sacrificed to idols. This hideous practice had been ongoing for some time. The Thyatira Christians allowed this heresy to occur, for which they were condemned by God. Believers who condone heresy and refuse to stand up against the Jezebels who peddle it are like the Thyatira saints. Jude exhorts all believers to rigorously combat theological error. He writes, "Beloved, when I gave all diligence to write unto you of the common salvation, it was needful for me to write unto you, and exhort you that ye should earnestly contend for the faith which was once delivered unto the saints. For there are certain men crept in unawares…" (Jude 3–4). Keep tight grips upon the faith, standing courageously against the Jezebels of this age who seek to undermine it.

The Sardis kind (3:1–6). Sardis Christians have the reputation of being fully alive, while they are stone dead. As with the Pharisees, the outer life of Sardis Christians conceals their true heart condition. Sardis church members are caught up in outward form. They pray, but without power; they worship, but their worship rises no higher than the ceiling; they sing, but they are just mouthing words. They are spiritually dead. Samson in the Old Testament is a picture of a Sardis Christian in the New Testament. Upon losing his power with God, he said, "I will go out as at other times before, and shake myself. And he knew not that the LORD had departed from him" (Judges 16:20 Webster). He did as he had done

125

before, but nothing happened. Are you a Samson, going through the religious motions, shaking yourself with nothing happening of any eternal consequence? If so, spiritual power has been lost without your knowing it, reducing you to a dry shadow of what you once were for Christ. To those of the Sardis disposition, Jesus says, "Repent."

The Laodicean kind (3:14–22). No good word could be uttered by our Lord on behalf of the Laodicean church, only condemnation. Saints of Laodicea were neither spiritually cold (literally meaning cold to the point of freezing) nor hot (literally meaning to the point of boiling), but lukewarm. Things that are lukewarm are often nauseating to drink or to eat. A fitting synonym for lukewarm in this context is indifference. Jesus frankly declares that He is sick to His stomach over the indifference saints of this fellowship display for spiritual things. What a cutting rebuke!

One spiritual trait that the Christian must not exhibit is neutrality—a complacent, satisfied, contented attitude with the status quo personally and in the church corporately. Guard the heart from indifference; keep stoking the fire; remain close to Christ and submissive so your faith does not degenerate into nominal Christianity void of delight, duty, discipline, or devotion. If such has happened, immediately repent and ignite the fire in the boiler of the heart for God.

The Philadelphia kind (3:7–8). The Philadelphia Christian represents the type of believer who is obedient, exhibiting unquestioned loyalty to Christ. Commendation is given to these saints by Christ: "Thou...hast kept my word, and hast not denied my name" (verse 8). That's a good epitaph. May you and I be worthy of its inscription upon our tombstone.

John Stott states, "If we want to convince Jesus Christ that we love Him, there is only one way to do so. It is neither to make protestations of our devotion, nor to work up feelings of affection toward Him, nor to sing hymns of personal piety, nor even to give ourselves to the service of humanity. It is to obey His commandments. Jesus demonstrated His love for the Father by His obedience ('I do as the Father has commanded me,' John 14:31); we must demonstrate our love for Christ by our obedience."[123] Obedience is the proof of the believer's love for Christ and was demonstrated by the Philadelphia Christians.

> I love Thee; I love Thee; I love Thee, my Lord.
> I love Thee, my Savior; I love Thee, my God.
> I love Thee, I love Thee, and that Thou doest know;
> But how much I love Thee my actions will show.[124]

The Corinth kind (2 Corinthians 13:5). Within the church are many who bear the name of Christ, who are card-toting members of the church, that are not saved. Such was the condition of some in the church at Corinth. The apostle Paul asked of them a question that is just as relevant for you to answer: "Examine yourselves, whether ye be in the faith; prove your own selves. Know ye not your own selves, how that Jesus Christ is in you, except ye be reprobates?" If you died today, are you absolutely positive God would permit your entrance into Heaven? If uncertain, stop right now and invite Jesus into your life as Lord and Savior; exchange the false hope for the real hope (Romans 10:9–13).

The Lord knows "where thou dwellest" (Revelation 2:13)—the kind of Christian you are. It's time you acknowledge the kind you are and, if you are like any cited in this Hot Button with whom God was displeased, repent and get back on track spiritually. Resolve to be a Philadelphia-type Christian.

ASK YOURSELF

For what was the Ephesus church condemned, and is it yet a present danger for the Christian?

Describe the Smyrna Christian.

Share an experience in which a stand taken for Christ cost you something.

Do you agree or disagree with the statement that the church resembles the Laodicean church of the first century; and, if so, in what ways?

Who is a Pergamos Christian?

Who are the Jezebels of this age, and what ought to be the Christian's response to them?

In what way is Samson an Old Testament type of the Sardis kind of Christian?

What is the meaning of Jesus' words: "Neither cold nor hot"?

What is the only church of Asia Minor not condemned for anything, but totally commended for everything?

What was the commendation this church received?

Who is the Corinth kind of church member?

20 David and Goliath

"And David said to Saul, Let no man's heart fail because of him; thy servant will go and fight with this Philistine."—1 Samuel 17:32.

Every now and again—not often, but sometimes—God brings us to a point of climax. That is the Great Divide in the life; from that point, we either go towards a more and more dilatory [sluggish] and useless type of Christian life, or we become more and more ablaze for the glory of God—My Utmost for His Highest.[125]—Oswald Chambers

We are more than conquerors through Him that loved us. We shall cast down the powers of darkness which are in the world by our faith and zeal and holiness. We shall win sinners to Jesus; we shall overturn false systems; we shall convert nations; for God is with us, and none shall stand before us.[126]—C. H. Spurgeon

The giant Goliath wanted someone from King Saul's army with whom to fight. The winner of that duel would determine whether the Philistines or the Israelites would be declared the victors. No one wanted to fight Goliath, who stood over nine feet tall and wore heavy battle armor—that is, not until a young man named David arrived, willing to do what the experienced soldiers in Saul's army were afraid to do. In facing this big challenge, David refused to let others discourage or stop him. He was determined from the get-go to do what God wanted him to do.

How can we do the big things that God wants us do? First Samuel 17 tells us how, through the example of David.

Think Big. David thought big long before he ever did big (verse 26). Think big about the things God wants you to do. Don't let anyone talk you out of doing what God puts in your heart to accomplish (verses 28–29). Has God put in your heart the desire to be a missionary, pastor, evangelist, student minister, or musician? Keep thinking big about doing it, even though it seems a long way off or impossible.

Talk Big. David talked some "big talk" assuring the king that because God was with him he would defeat Goliath, didn't he (verses 36–37)? In gist, David told the king, "It's in the bag. It's a done deal. I am going to defeat him because God is with me." That's "faith" kind of talking. Don't be afraid to talk big about what God has put in your heart to do. Joseph talked big about God's plan for his life. His brothers called him a dreamer, poking fun at him, but that didn't stop him. Others may laugh at you in disbelief when you tell them what God wants you to do, but keep walking in faith.

Believe Big. David not only thought big and talked big; he believed big (verses 45–46). He was confident that God would enable him to beat Goliath. Never doubt that God will help you to do what He tells you to do, regardless of how big the task appears. Believing big like this is what the Bible calls faith (Hebrews 11:6).

Do Big. To think big, talk big, and believe big is nothing, unless one does big. David did big (verses 48–50). David did what God put in his heart to do—he slew Goliath. Think big about what God wants you to do, talk big about it, believe big about it, but then do big about it. There are too many who think big, talk big, and believe big who never do big. Use this time of life to prepare for that time later in life when you will have the opportunity to do big things for God.[127]

ASK YOURSELF

What big task might God be asking you to accomplish?

Are you fearful of the negative response from others if you share God's leading? Why?

How did David handle the unbelief of others regarding his mission?

What task have you begun for God but stopped prior to completion? Why?

Isn't it time to finish it?

"Every day people who say it can't be done are being interrupted by people doing it."

21   The Consequence of One Sin

"Whatsoever a man soweth, that shall he also reap."—Galatians 6:7.

"Let him that thinketh he standeth take heed lest he fall."—1 Corinthians 10:12.

All the Devil's apples have worms.

If you yield to Satan in the least, he will carry you further and further till he has left you under a stupefied or terrified conscience—stupefied till thou hast lost all thy tenderness. A stone at the top of a hill, when it begins to roll down, ceases not till it comes to the bottom. Thou thinkest it is but yielding a little and so by degrees art carried on till thou hast sinned away all thy profession and all principles of conscience by the secret witchery of his temptations.[128]—Thomas Manton

Saul's failure to utterly destroy the Amalekites as God commanded led to his rejection as King of Israel (1 Samuel 15:23). Surely Saul had underestimated the consequences of just one sin, never dreaming it would cost him the throne of Israel. Students identify with Saul in that they equally are prone to overestimate the tolerance of God toward sin and underestimate its tragic consequences.

What might the act of just one sin produce in your life? *It can color the rest of your life*. Playing with sin is like playing with coal. It is impossible not to be colored with its nature. You may say, "Frank, this one thing wrong I do won't hurt me. Everybody is doing it. One beer won't hurt me. One snort won't hurt me. One visit to a pornographic website won't harm me. One act of sexual immorality won't injure me. Cheating one time on an exam won't hurt me."

You are wrong. Sin, regardless of its size or the number of times it is committed, does hurt you, and it colors the rest of life. King Saul will attest to this as indisputable.

It can addict (enslave) for all of your life. A Kentucky farmer maintained his field like a garden. A young man, in anger, sneaked into the field at night and sowed Johnson grass seed. In time, the grass sprouted and spread throughout the farmer's field. The farmer never learned of the culprit who sowed it. Years passed, and the young man who sowed the seed in the field married the farmer's daughter. Upon the death of his father-in-law, he inherited the farm. This man fought the unending battle of digging up the roots of that Johnson grass he had sown in his youth.

Sowing the seeds of alcohol, drugs, pornography, dishonesty, and immorality in the soul now may lead to a lifetime of digging them up by the roots. Youth is the planting stage of life; adulthood is the reaping stage. You will reap what you sow, perhaps for the rest of your life. "One sin," says C. H. Spurgeon, "can ruin a soul forever; it is not in the power of the human mind to grasp the infinity of evil that slumbereth in the bowels of one solitary sin."[129]

It can alter God's plan for your life. Saul was God's choice to rule Israel, but one sin thwarted that from occurring. Moses was God's choice to lead the Israelites into the Promised Land, but one sin prevented it. Samson was God's man to judge Israel, but after twenty years, one sin forced him to step down. Likewise only one sin can cause God to alter His perfect plan for your life. Don't possibly forfeit God's foremost plan by yielding to one sin.

It can spoil the testimony for life. It takes one sin only a few minutes to tear down the strong reputation and testimony that took years to construct.

It can shorten life. Ananias and Sapphira had life cut short due to one sin (Acts 5:10). Achan's one sin shortened his life (Joshua 7:20-25). The Apostle John states that there is a "sin unto death" (1 John 5:16). The consumption of alcohol shortens one's life; the use of drugs shortens life; tobacco use shortens life; perverted sexual lifestyles shorten life. Mark it down—one sin may lead to a life cut short.

It can condemn the soul to Hell for eternity. The only sin that separates man from God for eternity is that of unbelief. Jesus declared, "He that believeth on him is not condemned: but he that believeth not is condemned already, because he hath not believed in the name of the only begotten Son of God" (John 3:18). In order to go to Hell, one does not have to live a life of grave sin; he only needs to neglect Christ as Lord and Savior. If you are not a Christian, right now turn from sin and embrace Christ as your Lord and Savior (Romans 10:9–13).

One sin confessed may be forgiven. Solomon states, "He that covereth his sins shall not prosper: but whoso confesseth and forsaketh *them* shall have mercy" (Proverbs 28:13). Either you allow God to deal with your sin, or you will have to deal with it. He stands ever ready to forgive and cleanse of whatever sin you acknowledge with a repentant heart (1 John 1:9; Hebrews 8:12). Sin confessed is forgiven; however, its consequences may be unalterable. Never forget this truth!

As a little thorn causes a great blister, a little moth destroys a great garment, and a small fox destroys a great vine, what you count as a little sin, committed but one time, can bring irreparable damage to your life.

One dropped ball defined the entire span of Mickey Owen's eighty-nine years of life, according to his obituary in *The State* on July 16, 2005. This infamous dropped third strike occurred in the 1941 World Series when his team, the Brooklyn Dodgers, played the New York Yankees. Brooklyn had a 4-3 lead in Game 4 with two outs in the last inning when Owen dropped the third strike to Tommy Henrich. This passed ball gave the Yankee's new life, and they went on to score four runs, winning the game. It is interesting to note that little was said about Owen hitting the first home run as a pinch-hitter in an All Star game in 1941 or the fact that he played in four All Star games. The whole of his life, according to the obituary, was defined by *one dropped ball*.

How would you like your life to be *defined* by one dropped ball? Sadly, our life's successes can be clouded with one failure. David's great accomplishments for God in being King and in writing many of the Psalms are overshadowed by his one dropped ball with Bathsheba. Samson's successes for God are overshadowed by his dropped ball regarding Delilah. John Mark's successes for God are overshadowed by his dropped ball in deserting Paul at Pamphylia. Peter's great accomplishments for the Kingdom of God are overshadowed by his dropped ball in Caiaphas' palace. As with these, even so it is with us that one *dropped ball*—one flagrant sin can cast a cloud over all our many spiritual successes and life's achievements. Unfair as this is, nonetheless, that's how it is. One sin may color all the rest of life.

What do you want the legacy of your life to be? Certainly not a single *dropped ball*. Therefore, exhibit diligence to make sure that such is not the case, by holding yourself accountable to God and to a friend in whom you can confide. God is always merciful and loving to forgive and forget the *dropped balls* in our life. Sadly, man is not. If you have dropped the ball, He stands ready to forgive and restore. If you know another who has stumbled, be "Jesus in the flesh" unto him, granting forgiveness.

As a young person, you are building a legacy for which you will be ever remembered by colleagues, friends, employees and family.

C. H. Spurgeon's prayer on deliverance from sins:

136

"Lord, save me from my sins. By the name of Jesus I am encouraged thus to pray. Save me from my past sins, that the habit of them may not hold me captive. Save me from my constitutional sins, that I may not be the slave of my own weaknesses. Save me from the sins which are continually under my eye, that I may not lose my horror of them. Save me from secret sins—sins unperceived by me from my want of light. Save me from sudden and surprising sins; let me not be carried off my feet by a rush of temptation. Save me, Lord, from every sin. Let not any iniquity have dominion over me.

"You alone can do this. I cannot snap my own chains or slay my own enemies. You know temptation, for You were tempted. You know sin, for You did bear the weight of it. You know how to help me in my hour of conflict; You can save me from sinning and save me when I have sinned. It is promised in Thy very name that You will do this, and I pray, let me this day verify the prophecy. Let me not give way to temper or pride or despondency or any form of evil; but do, O Lord, save me unto holiness of life, that the name of Jesus may be glorified in me abundantly."[130]

ASK YOURSELF

Do you consider the outcome of a wrong act prior to doing it?

How might doing so spare you heartache and sorrow?

What "Johnson grass" are you trying to dig up by the roots?

Has the act of one sin committed one time resulted in an outcome never imagined?

According to 1 John 1:9, how may sin be forgiven?

Have you dropped the ball? If so, go to God in repentance, and He will forgive.

What preventative steps may be taken to insure that it doesn't occur again?

Do you believe one dropped ball can color the rest of a person's life? Why or why not?

What do you want the legacy of your life to be?

Take a moment and make Spurgeon's prayer cited above a personal prayer.

22   The Deadly Danger of Drifting

"So we must listen very carefully to the truth we have heard, or we may drift away from it."—Hebrews 2:1 NLT

Without an anchor, a "parked" boat will drift. In a similar way, unless we are anchored in the Word, we can easily slip away from a close relationship with God. The unsecured vessel may float quickly to a new location, whereas a spiritual change can occur slowly and without our knowledge. Such "slippage" is often gradual. It's easy to adjust to each slight shift and become accustomed to [an increasingly] superficial Christian walk. Spiritual drifting usually indicates living outside of God's will.[131]—Charles Stanley

The easiest thing in the world to do is to drift; it requires no effort at all. To drift spiritually, all one has to do is simply to do nothing with his or her faith. Many students who were giants for God no longer are, due to spiritual carelessness. What are the spiritual rafts that must be avoided, lest they drift believers downstream away from God?

Students drift from God due to a false faith. John states that this was the reason for the departure of some from Christ in the church of his day (1 John 2:19). Apart from the sure Anchor of Salvation, Jesus Christ, it is impossible not to drift. Is your faith the real genuine deal or a counterfeit imitation?

Drifting occurs due to religious surfing. You don't need to be nosing around in other religions looking for something better. You have the best and that which is true, so stick to it. Hear the admonition of Paul: "Hold fast the form of sound words, which thou hast heard of me, in faith and love which is in Christ Jesus. That good thing which was committed unto thee keep by the Holy Ghost which dwelleth in us" (2 Timothy 1:13–14). Allowing non-Christian religious seeds to be sown in the mind will result in devastating spiritual shipwreck. You have the Truth; there is no need to search among heretical faiths for it.

Drifting among students occurs due to wrong friends. Friends will be an asset or a deficit, a plus or a minus, a help or a hindrance to your walk with God. Select friends cautiously and prayerfully, for no other factor outside of one's parents influences life to a greater degree.

Friendships are so powerful an influence that they impact our lives in at least three ways. First, we become *like* them. Goethe said, "Tell me with whom thou art found, and I will tell thee who thou art." We become like those with whom we associate. Pure and clean water passing through a dirty pipe will become dirty. Does placing a good apple next to a rotten apple change the nature of that rotten apple? Certainly not, but the rotten apple changes the nature of the good one. Many clean and promising youths have fallen into the mire and filth of sin due to wrong associations.

Second, we become known *as* them. A man is known by the company he keeps. People are prone to judge a person based upon the company he or she entertains.

Third, our future will be affected *by* them. Go to any prison, reformatory or drug rehab center, and it is doubtful that you will find one youth who wouldn't say a friend played a role in his being there. Visit the graves of the young in the cemeteries of the world, and an honest epitaph etched upon the tombstones of far too many would include the words: "I'm here due to a friend." Your future good or evil is affected by your friends. Now is the time to evaluate friendships and change them if they fail the biblical test (Psalm 119:63; Proverbs 13:20).

Drifting occurs due to living on past spiritual highs. The spiritual emotional high experienced at summer camp or revival won't last long. You can't live on it—it can't be done. A fresh encounter with God daily is an absolute imperative if you are to progress rather than digress spiritually. The Israelites in the wilderness were to gather manna daily. If they sought to save the manna for the next day, spoilage would occur. In this, I see the principle of disciplined quiet time. Spiritual manna awaits the believer who is hungry enough to come to the table daily to receive it. Spiritual life is sustained by feasting regularly upon God's Word.

Drifting occurs among students due to a favorite sin. Dr. G. Campbell Morgan was pastor of a church in London. A young man came to him and told him he had been living a dissipated life and that now he wanted to become a Christian. He was received into the church and didn't miss a single service for several months. Then he dropped out of the church, and Dr. Morgan went to see him. He said to him, "I have come to tell you how much we have been missing you here at the church."

The young man said, "There's no use for you to talk to me about your Christianity. I have tried it, and it's a failure."

Then Dr. Morgan seized a number of lewd pictures on the mantel and threw them into the fire, saying as he did it, "How can you ever expect to be a real Christian unless you burn your bridges behind you?"[132]

This certainly is right advice for all. If you are to live for Christ without wavering, the coattails of former sin must be severed permanently. The sin that you are unwilling to forsake will be the sin that brings you down.

Students drift due to neglect of God's house. Forsake the church, and your boat is adrift. As mentioned in chapter 6, because they have shallow roots, gigantic redwoods intertwine their roots with other redwoods in the forest, enabling them to stand tall amid storms and high winds. You have shallow roots spiritually which must be intertwined with the roots of other believers for stability and strength. A chunk of coal separated from hot coals will gradually lose its warmth—likewise for the Christian who neglects the assembling with believers regularly at church.

Drifting occurs due to spiritual laziness. "I went by the field of the lazy man, And...Thorns had grown up everywhere....The stone wall had fallen down" (Proverbs 24:30–31 NIRV). Solomon portrays in this verse a towering strong wall that, due to neglect of its owner's care (laziness), fell to the ground. Failure to care for the "strong wall" of your walk with Jesus through the disciplines of prayer, Bible study, worship, confession, and witnessing will likewise lead to its collapse.

Students drift due to distractions. School, sports, work, dating, relationships, entertainment, and clubs or fraternities are potential distractions in living for Jesus. Demas failed to handle the distractions he faced successfully and drifted from his first love for Christ (2 Timothy 4:10). Recognize potential distractions and carefully protect your walk with Christ, lest your end be like that of Demas.

ASK YOURSELF

What do you count to be the biggest causes for drifting from the Lord?

How can preventative measures be enacted to counter such causes?

Are you drifting downstream away from allegiance to and love for Christ; and, if so, what has prompted it?

Reflect on how good it was to live near Christ, and return to your first love for Him.

23   Failure Is Not Final; God Gives Second Chances

"And Peter remembered the word of Jesus, which said unto him, Before the cock crow, thou shalt deny me thrice. And he went out, and wept bitterly."—Matthew 26:75.

Our yesterdays hold broken and irreversible things for us. It is true that we have lost opportunities that will never return, but God can transform this destructive anxiety into a constructive thoughtfulness for the future. Let the past rest, but let it rest in the sweet embrace of Christ. Leave the broken, irreversible past in His hands, and step out into the invincible future with Him.[133]—Oswald Chambers

There is no remembrance of our follies; He [God] does not cherish ill thoughts of us, but He pardons and loves as well after the offense as before it.[134]—C. H. Spurgeon

Can it be possible that sin, such sin as mine, can be forgiven, forgiven altogether, and forever? Hell is my portion as a sinner— there is no possibility of my escaping from it while sin remains upon me. Can the load of guilt be uplifted, the crimson stain removed? Can the adamantine stones of my prison house ever be loosed from their mortises or the doors be lifted from their hinges? Jesus tells me that I may yet be clear. Forever blessed be the revelation of atoning love which not only tells me that pardon is possible, but that it is secured to all who rest in Jesus.[135]—C. H. Spurgeon

All have experienced failure in their spiritual walk. In Scripture, one finds a long list of those who failed.

David failed. He committed adultery with Bathsheba (2 Samuel 11:4).

Moses failed. He killed an Egyptian and tried to conceal the act (Exodus 2:12).

Demas failed. He deserted the Lord for love of the world (2 Timothy 4:10).

Elijah failed. This spiritual giant failed God at Jezreel when he fled Jezebel (1 Kings 19:3).

And Peter failed. He denied the Lord three distinct times (Matthew 26:75). Failure happens to the best of saints, and with the failure comes loss of peace, power, and oneness with Christ.

What are you to do when you fail and fall into sin?

Recognize it. Finger the sin and accept full responsibility. Don't play the blame game. Own up to it.

Repent of it. Immediately confess the wrong act to God and sincerely ask His forgiveness. The only sin God refuses to forgive is the sin we refuse to confess.

Release it. Let go of it. Upon God's forgiveness regarding the sin, forgive yourself and move on. Refuse to allow Satan to hold your conscience captive to an act that God has erased, blotted out, and forgotten (Isaiah 43:25; Hebrews 8:12, 10:17; Micah 7:19).

Rebound from it. Oswald Chambers said, "Never let the sense of failure corrupt your new action."[136] He was saying you must get up, dust yourself off, and press on, unhampered by the sin of yesterday so you can fulfill God's plan for today.

Peter failed, but upon confession, he was restored to become the great preacher at Pentecost where over 3,000 souls were saved (Acts 2). David failed, but upon confession, he was restored to write many of the instructive and inspiring psalms in the

Bible. Failure certainly doesn't have to be final. Don't let it be for you.

In the 1929 Rose Bowl, Roy, a player for Southern California, ran the football back the wrong way. A teammate tackled him just before he scored a touchdown for the wrong team. At halftime, Roy sat alone in the locker room amid speculation of teammates as to what the coach would say to him. Finally, just prior to the end of halftime, the coach announced that all who started the game would start the second half. Roy remained seated and sobbing, prompting the coach to say, "Come on Roy."

Roy replied, "I can't coach. I embarrassed the team and myself. I can never face the crowd again."

The coach responded, "The game is only half over." What a coach! But greater still is a Savior who tells you when you have failed that the game of life is not over, that there are opportunities in the second half to do better. He is the God of the second chance.

Jesus instructs us to forgive others "seventy times seven" (Matthew 18:22). That's a lot of "second" chances. Certainly if He taught that His disciples ought to do this, He does so even more perfectly.

ASK YOURSELF

When have you last failed God?

What did you do to reconcile (get right) with Him?

Do you find it difficult rebounding from sin? Why?

Is it hard to believe that God will absolutely and totally wipe clean the slate of personal sin upon request from a broken and contrite heart? Why?

Have you ever identified with Roy in a spiritual sense? Do you presently?

In what way(s) does the coach remind you of God?

Describe a time when God gave you a second chance.

Are second chances conditional; and, if so, in what way?

Do you doubt God's willingness to give you a second chance now?

Hear God speak to your heart, saying, "The game is only half over. I forgive you. I want you right back out there in the second half. Don't allow past failure to hinder future potential. Now get out there and make a difference."

24   The Goal-Line Stand

"I will arise and go to my father, and will say unto him, Father, I have sinned against heaven, and before thee....And he arose, and came to his father."—Luke 15:18, 20.

You're going to be tempted by the flesh. Run away. You're going to be tempted by the Devil. Stand up and fight with the Word of God in your hand, the sword of the Spirit, and the shield of faith wherewith you shall be able to quench all the fiery darts of the evil one (Ephesians 6:16). And as to the world round about you, be not conformed, but day by day, ask God to pour you into the mold of Christ.[137]—Donald Grey Barnhouse

Don't give Satan another inch of ground in your life. Draw a line in the sand and say, "Enough is enough." Then take back all Satan took, in the authority of Jesus' name.

During football season, when the opposing team is on the one-yard line seeking to score, the great cry from fans that reverberates throughout the stadium is: "Hold that line!" You may have let them drive the ball 90 yards, played sluggishly, missed key tackles, and made senseless mistakes resulting in penalties; but, at the one-yard line, you set your cleats firmly in the sod and determine enough is enough.

Life is like football in this regard. You get pushed back, knocked down, and run over by mistakes you make; and just as the enemy is about to deliver the final blow, you set your cleats in the sod at the goal line and say, "No further!"

Mel Trotter, an alcoholic, did just this on January 19, 1897. On that day, he staggered into the Pacific Garden Mission so intoxicated that he didn't even know his own name. Mel's mother was a godly woman, but his dad was an alcoholic bartender. Mel couldn't keep a job and was a hopeless alcoholic at age twenty. In an effort to overcome the craving for alcohol, he was hospitalized, but to no avail. He married in 1891. At the end of one of his ten-day drinking sprees, Trotter returned home only to discover that his two-year-old son had died. Deeply grieved, he promised his wife never to touch alcohol again—a promise short-lived, for two hours later he staggered home drunk.

In a Chicago winter, Trotter, now aged twenty-seven, decided to commit suicide by jumping into the icy waters of Lake Michigan. In walking toward Lake Michigan, he passed the Pacific Garden Mission and entered, only to hear Harry Monroe (converted alcoholic) sharing his testimony of deliverance from alcohol. That night Mel Trotter was saved.

Trotter later became the director of a new rescue mission in Grand Rapids, Michigan, where he served for forty years. By the time of his death, Trotter had established sixty-seven other rescue missions across the nation.[138]

Mel Trotter, though beaten down by Satan for ninety-nine yards, said, "No further," and had his victorious "goal-line stand."

You are not alone at the one-yard line. You have been beaten down but not defeated. There are not enough demons in Hell to drag you over the one-yard line into eternal bleakness, hopelessness, and Hell, if you cling to Jesus Christ.

Peter gave up much ground to the enemy by denying the Lord three times, but at the one-yard line, strength from the Lord was tapped to "hold that line" and not let Satan score a sweeping victory.

Samson, due to his strength, was picked to win the day; but carelessness led to weakness, and this giant was pushed back to the one-yard line by Delilah. But at the one-yard line, Samson cried, "O Lord GOD, remember me, I pray thee, and strengthen me, I pray thee, only this once, O God, that I may be at once avenged of the Philistines for my two eyes" (Judges 16:28). Needless to say, with God on his side, he held the line.

David fumbled the ball big time with Bathsheba and let Satan beat him to a pulp, but he triumphed in the Lord in a goal-line stand (Psalm 51:1–17).

Joseph's one-yard-line stand is one of the greatest in the Bible. Mrs. Potiphar made daily seductive advances to this handsome youth, determined to rob him of his purity (Genesis 39:7, 10). Finally the moment came when he was at the one-yard line. His purity and walk with God were on the line. He made an unforgettable goal-line stand, refusing to let her make any further advancement, and won the day (Genesis 39:11–13). The knockout punch came when Joseph told her, "There is none greater in this house than I; neither hath he kept back any thing from me but thee, because thou art his wife: how then can I do this great wickedness, and sin against God?" (Genesis 39:9).

You have a one-yard-line stand to make against sexual impurity, drugs, pornography, alcohol, marital infidelity, or dishonesty. You have been pushed back, overrun, outplayed, and fooled by the play calls of Satan. He has beaten you hand over fist to this moment. Now your back is to the wall, and you must take the goal-line stand or else suffer utter defeat.

Don't quit. Don't despair. Don't allow what you have done, the defeats you have suffered, to break your spirit, resulting in an attitude of hopelessness. You can win. With others, you can make an unforgettable goal-line stand that will change everything.

Make a goal-line stand now. Have an enough-is-enough attitude toward how Satan has been defeating you and robbing joy, peace, and fulfillment from your life. God will stand with you as you stand against Satan; with God on your side, you "outnumber and outplay" the opponent, regardless of who or what he throws at you.

You indeed can do all things through Christ who strengthens you (Philippians 4:13). On your own you will fail, but with Jesus, you will prevail. Right now, decide to stop being beaten down by Satan, entangled and/or entrapped by some sinful indulgence, and robbed of what God intended.

The prodigal son of Luke 15 faced a goal-line stand in the pigpens of a "far country" (far from peace, purpose, potential, purity, and parent). This teen, after being driven further and further down the field of life by the great opponent, Satan, awakened at the one-yard line determined to stop his retreat. He held the line the moment he declared, "I will arise and go to my father, and will say unto him, Father, I have sinned against heaven, and before thee" (Luke 15:18), and when he actually did so (verse 20).

You can come back from the brink of utter defeat, as this youth did. You can have a goal-line stand and reverse directions. You do not have to remain as you are or where you are. Things can be different. You can change. You can come back from the far country to a loving, forgiving God.

Hold that Line. Don't allow the enemy of the soul to push you back any further and eventually take you over the goal line to even greater misery, heartache, and Hell. It's time for you to make a goal-line stand, one which you will never regret. Multitudes of Christians in the stands and on the sideline are cheering for you to hold that line. Millions have made this stand stopping Satan's advances, which proves it can be done. Do now as the prodigal son; get up and come to God without delay![139]

ASK YOURSELF

Do you identify with Mel Trotter, Joseph, or the prodigal son; and, if so, in what ways?

How did each of these individuals make a goal line stand against the attack of Satan?

What would be your counsel to those who ask how they can reverse the direction of their lives spiritually and morally?

Do you need to make a goal line stand right now and reverse directions?

Endnotes

[1] Francis Schaeffer. *A Christian View of Spirituality.* (Wheaton: Crossway Books, 1982), 258.

[2] W. R. Moody, Ed., *Record of Christian Work—Volume XVII.* (New York: Fleming H. Revell Company, 1898), 573.

[3] C. H. Spurgeon. *Morning and Evening.* (Rose-Shire, Scotland: Christian Focus Publications, 1994), November 26.

[4] Oswald Chambers. *My Utmost for His Highest.* (Grand Rapids: Discovery House Publishers, 1993), December 27.

[5] William Jensen, Compiler. *Pursued by Love Everlasting.* (Eugene, Or.: Harvest House Publishers, 1999), unnumbered pages.

[6] Michael Combs. "Not for Sale" (CD). Lamb Lover Music.

[7] "Christian Student Quits Choir When Forced to Sing." www.christianresponsealerts.com, accessed February 24, 2012.

[8] Paul Tan. Encyclopedia of 7700 Illustrations (Rockville, Md.: Assurance Publishers, 1979), 243.

[9] "Christian Quotes on Courage." dailychristianquote.com/dcqcourage.html, accessed November 29, 2011.

[10] William Francis Collier. *History of the British Empire (1870).* (Edinburg and New York: T. Nelson & Sons, 1876), 124.

[11] Contributed by Dr. Nina Gunter who got it from veteran missionary Louise Robinson Chapman (Africa: 1920–1940).

[12] Donald S. Whitney. *Spiritual Disciplines of the Christian Life.* (Colorado Springs: NavPress, 2002), 26.

[13] William Lane Craig. *Reasonable Faith.* (Wheaton: Crossway Books, 1994), 300.

[14] Cited in "Preach the Word: Back to the Basics Part I: The Morning Watch," www.preachtheword.com/sermon/b2b01.shtml, accessed December 6, 2011.

[15] E. M. Bounds. *Power through Prayer.* (Scotts Valley, Cal.: CreateSpace, 2009), 50.

[16] D. L. Moody, *Pleasures and Profit of Bible Study.* (Grand Rapids: Fleming Revell Publishers, 1895), 79. [The first five *P*s are A. T. Pierson's; the sixth is the author's.]

[17] Adrian Rogers. "How to Have a Meaningful Quiet Time." Lwf.org, accessed March 12, 2011.

[18] C. H. Spurgeon. *Morning and Evening,* October 12.

[19] Christian Prayer Quotations. www.christian-prayer-quotes.christian-attorney.net/, accessed November 30, 2011.

[20] Ibid.

[21] Ibid.

[22] W. W. Wiersbe. *The Bible Exposition Commentary.* (Wheaton: Victor Books, 1996), Luke 18:1

[23] John MacArthur. *The Keys to Spiritual Growth.* (Wheaton: Crossway Books, 1991), 123.

[24] Adrian Rogers. "The Privilege of Prayer." Lwf.org, accessed November 30, 2011.

Endnotes

[25] Curtis Hutson, Ed., *Great Preaching on Prayer.* (Murfreesboro, Tenn.: Sword of the Lord Publishers, 1988), 45.

[26] Stephen Olford. *I'll Take the High Road.* (Grand Rapids: Zondervan Publishing House, 1969), 31.

[27] "21 Great Quotes about Church."
http://www.whatchristianswanttoknow.com/21-great-quotes-about-church/#ixzz27x0WkrAS.

[28] David Kinnaman cited by Greg Kandra, "You Lost Me." Why teens leave church. www.patheos.com/.../2011/10/.../you-lost-me-why-teens-leave-church, accessed October 21, 2011.

[29] Ray Comfort, Ed., *The Evidence Bible.* (Gainesville, Fl.: Bridge-Logos Publishers, 2002), 456.

[30] Adrian Rogers. "Unwrapping Your Spiritual Gifts." Lwf.org, accessed December 5, 2011.

[31] C. H. Spurgeon. "Our Gifts and How to Use Them." www.biblebb.com/files/spurgeon/1080.htm, accessed December 6, 2011.

[32] Young Ladies Christian Fellowship. "Overview of Spiritual Gifts." ylcf.org/you/spiritual-gift/overview/, accessed December 5, 2011.

[33] "Spiritual Gifts Chart." www.preceptaustin.org/spiritual_gifts_chart.htm, accessed December 6, 2011.

[34] "Discerning and Using Your Spiritual Gift." www.olivetbaptistokc.com/subpage18.html, accessed December 5, 2011.

[35] John Piper. "Spiritual Gifts," March 15, 1981 (Morning), Bethlehem Baptist Church. www.soundofgrace.com/piper81/031581m.htm, accessed December 6, 2011.

[36] Bill Bright. *The Holy Spirit: The Key to Supernatural Living.* (San Bernardino: Here's Life, 1980), 218.

[37] Matthew Henry. *Matthew Henry Concise Commentary on the Bible* (1 Corinthians 12:1–11). mhc.biblecommenter.com/1_corinthians/12.htm, accessed December 6, 2011.

[38] *Believer's Study Bible.* (Nashville: Thomas Nelson, 1997 electronic ed.) (1 Corinthians 12:8).

[39] J. V. McGee. *Thru the Bible Commentary.* (Nashville: Thomas Nelson, 1997 electronic ed.) (1 Co 12:8).

[40] J. Courson. *Jon Courson's Application Commentary.* (Nashville: Thomas Nelson, 2003), 1070.

[41] J. MacArthur. *The MacArthur Study Bible.* (Nashville: Word Pub., 1997 electronic edition), (1 Corinthians 12:8).

[42] Courson, 973.

[43] W. Barclay, Ed. *The Daily Study Bible Series, Rev. Ed., The Letter to the Romans.* (Philadelphia: The Westminster Press, 2000), 161.

[44] C. Peter Wagoner. *Your Spiritual Gifts Can Help Your Church Grow.* (Ventura, California: Gospel Light, 2005), 191.

[45] Wiersbe, *The Bible Exposition Commentary,* Romans 12:3.

[46] Lewis Drummond. *The Canvas Cathedral.* (Nashville: Thomas Nelson, 2002), 65–66.

[47] Bill Gothard. "Student Leadership | Spiritual Gifts: Part 2 | Liberty University." www.liberty.edu › Faith & Service › Student Leadership, accessed December 6, 2011.

Endnotes

[48] R. Towns and E. L. Towns. *Women Gifted for Ministry: How to Discover and Practice Your Spiritual Gifts.* (Nashville: Thomas Nelson, 2001), 117.

[49] C. H. Spurgeon. "Our Gifts and How to Use Them."

[50] William Shakespeare. *Richard III,* Act 5, Scene 3.

[51] A. T. Robertson. *Paul and the Intellectuals.* (Nashville: Broadman,1959), 98.

[52] Don Whitney. *How Can I Be Sure I'm A Christian?* (Colorado Springs: NavPress, 1994), Foreword.

[53] Tullian Tchividjian. *Do I Know God?* (Portland: Multnomah Press,2007), 37.

[54] Whitney, *How Can I Be Sure I'm A Christian?*, Foreword.

[55] R. C. Sproul. *Essential Truths of the Christian Faith.* (Wheaton: Tyndale, 1992), 32.

[56] John R. Rice. *Rice Reference Bible.* (Nashville: Nelson Publishing, 1981), xii.

[57] C. H. Spurgeon. *Morning and Evening,* September 23 (morning entry).

[58] Ibid., December 20.

[59] Jason Gray. "Remind Me Who I Am," 2011.

[60] Adrian Rogers. "How Do I Know If I'm Saved?" lwf.org, accessed June 16, 2011.

[61] Whitney, *How Can I Be Sure I'm A Christian?*, 27.

[62] Ibid., 20.

[63] C. H. Spurgeon. *Metropolitan Tabernacle Pulpit: Vol. 63*, "Assurance Sought." (Pasadena, Tx: Pilgrim Publications, 1980), 21.

[64] Homer L. Cox. "It's Real." 1907. www.cyberhymnal.org/htm/i/t/s/its_real.htm, accessed June 16, 2011.

[65] Spurgeon, *Morning and Evening,* April 21.

[66] Arthur Bennett, Ed. *The Valley of Vision.* (Carlisle, Pa.: Banner of Truth, 1975/2002), 217.

[67] Cited in The Pastor's Forum: Sunday, June 12, 2011. pastorforum.blogspot.com/.../sunday-june-12-2011-promise-power-a..., accessed November 29, 2011.

[68] C. H. Spurgeon. *Faith's Checkbook.* (New Kensington, Pa.: Whitaker House, 2002), November 10 entry.

[69] dailychristianquote.com/dcqsin.html, accessed November 21, 2011.

[70] Spurgeon, *Morning and Evening,* May 03.

[71] Spurgeon, *Faith's Checkbook,* November 10.

[72] "Christian Quotes on Christians Being Ready to Engage the Enemy." dailychristianquote.com/dcqspiritwarfare.html, accessed November 29, 2011.

[73] Courson, 1265.

[74] John MacArthur. *Why Believe the Bible?* (Ventura, Cal.: Regal, 2007), 143–144.

[75] Courson, Matthew 6: 13.

[76] Spurgeon, *Morning and Evening,* November 3.

Endnotes

[77] James Mahoney. *Journey into Fullness.* (Nashville: Broadman Press, 1974), 54.

[78] John Stott. "Langham Partnership Daily Thought," www.langhampartnership.org, accessed November 4, 2011.

[79] Horatius Bonar. *Words to Winners of Souls.* (Phillipsburg, NJ.: P & R Publishing, 1995), 23–24.

[80] drboborr.blogspot.com/2010/10/will-you-rescue-me.html, accessed April 4, 2011.

[81] William Fay. *Share Jesus without Fear.* (Nashville: Broadman and Holman Publishers, 1999), 143.

[82] Anonymous. smallchurchmusic.com/Lyrics, accessed November 12, 2011.

[83] Bonar, 23–24.

[84] "Honduras Jail Fire Tragedy," www.Allvoices.com, accessed February 24, 2012.

[85] "Inspiring Quotes to Live By," www.soulwinning.info/gs/quotes.htm. Accessed November 29, 2011.

[86] L. R. Scarborough. *With Christ after the Lost.* (Nashville: Broadman Press, 1952), 43-44.

[87] E. M. Harrison. *How to Win Souls.* (Wheaton: Van Kamper Press, 1952), 23.

[88] Gene Bartlett. *The Baptist Hymnal*, "Set My Soul Afire," (Nashville: The Broadman Press, 1975), #302.

[89] Fred Barlow. "Travail for Souls" (Murfreesboro, Tenn.: The Sword of the Lord, 8 Oct. 2004), 1.

[90] C. H. Spurgeon. *Spurgeon's Sermons on Soulwinning.* (Grand Rapids: Kregal Publications, 1995), 33.

[91] Shelton Smith, Ed., *Great Preaching on Christ, Vol. 19* (Murfreesboro, Tenn.: Sword of the Lord Publishers, 2002), 175.

[92] Adrian Rogers. *The Passion of Christ and the Purpose of Life.* (Wheaton: Crossway Books, 2005), 67.

[93] Barclay, *The Revelation of John*, 142.

[94] "Inspiring Quotes to Live By," accessed November 29, 2011.

[95] John Borek, Danny Lovett, Elmer L. Towns. *The Good Book on Leadership: Case Studies from the Bible,* (Nashville: Broadman and Holman Publishers, 2005), 225.

[96] Ibid., 222.

[97] John MacArthur. *In the Footsteps of Faith: Lessons from the Lives of Great Men* (electronic ed.) (1998). (Wheaton: Crossway Books), 7.

[98] "Inspirational Christian Quotes by the Puritans," www.spurgeongems.org/iquotes.htm, accessed November 29, 2011.

[99] Adrian Rogers. *Unveiling the End Times in Our Time.* (Nashville: Broadman Press, 2004), 64–65.

[100] Spurgeon, *Metropolitan Tabernacle Pulpit,* "The Necessity of Regeneration," November 29, 1874.

[101] Warren Wiersbe. *On Being a Servant of God.* (Grand Rapids: Baker Books, 1993), 47.

[102] C. H. Spurgeon. *Morning and Evening,* December 27.

[103] F. E. Marsh. *1,000 Bible Study Outlines.* (Grand Rapids: Kregel Publications, 1970), 30.

[104] Ibid.

[105] Lewis Carroll. *Alice in Wonderland.* (Digital Scanning, Inc., 2007), 180.

[106] Max Lucado and T. A. Gibbs. *Grace for the Moment: Inspirational Thoughts for Each Day of the Year.* (Nashville: J. Countryman, 2000), 218.

[107] John MacArthur. *Reckless Faith.* (Wheaton: Victor Books, 1973), 190.

[108] Henry Blackaby, *Experiencing God*. (Nashville: Broadman and Holman, 2008), 194.

[109] Spurgeon, *Metropolitan Tabernacle Pulpit,* "The Holy Ghost—The Great Teacher," November 18, 1855.

[110] C. H. Spurgeon. *Lectures to My Students.* (Grand Rapids: Zondervan, 1970), 26.

[111] Ibid., 30.

[112] Ibid.

[113] "George Washington Truett," www.wilderness-cry.net/bible_study/bios/truett.html, accessed November 5, 2011.

[114] Spurgeon, *Lectures to My Students,* 30.

[115] John Stott, "Langham Partnership Daily Thought," November 7, 2011.

[116] Spurgeon. *Lectures to My Students,* "Ascension of Christ." http://www.biblebb.com/files/spurgeon/0982.htm, assessed May 28, 2009.

[117] Mary G. Brainard. "The Congregationalist," 1869; arranged by Philip P. Bliss in *Gospel Hymns No. 3,* circa 1876.

[118] "Christian Quotes on Fear," dailychristianquote.com/dcqfear.html, accessed December 1, 2011.

[119] Ibid.

[120] Spurgeon, *Faith's Checkbook,* November 30.

[121] Ibid., December 2.

[122] John Stott. "Langham Partnership Daily Thought," November 3, 2011, # 570.

[123] John Stott. *Christ the Liberator.* (Downers Grove: IVP, 1971), 39.

[124] Anonymous. "My Jesus I love Thee." (Jeremiah Ingalls Christian Harmony, 1805).

[125] Chambers, December 2

[126] Spurgeon. *Morning and Evening,* December 3.

[127] Oral Roberts, adapted from a 1974 sermon on television.

[128] dailychristianquote.com/dcqsin.html, accessed November 21, 2011.

[129] Spurgeon, *Metropolitan Tabernacle Pulpit,* "Particular Redemption," February 28, 1858.

[130] Spurgeon, *Faith's Checkbook,* October 21.

[131] Charles Stanley. "Warning against Spiritual Drifting," "In Touch Daily Devotional," April 14, 2008.

[132] W. Herschel Ford. *Simple Sermons on the Christian Life.* (Grand Rapids: Zondervan Publishing House, 1962), 62.

[133] Chambers, December 31.

[134] C. H. Spurgeon. *Morning and Evening,* December 3.

[135] C. H. Spurgeon. *Morning and Evening,* November 27.

[136] Chambers, February 18.

[137] Donald Grey Barnhouse. "How to Overcome Temptation." www.lwf.org/site/NewsArticle. accessed September 30, 2012.

[138] "Mel Trotter Delivered from Booze." chrisfieldblog.com/2009/01/19/mel-trotter, accessed September 30, 2012.

[139] Inspired and based upon C. M. Ward's sermon, "The One-Yard Line," 1965.